Simple Lessons Learned Along The Way

Craig Wagganer

1 Cor. 15:3-4
Craig

WESTBOW
PRESS®
A DIVISION OF THOMAS NELSON
& ZONDERVAN

Copyright © 2015 Craig Wagganer.

All rights reserved. No part of this book may be used or reproduced by any means, graphic, electronic, or mechanical, including photocopying, recording, taping or by any information storage retrieval system without the written permission of the author except in the case of brief quotations embodied in critical articles and reviews.

This book is a work of non-fiction. Unless otherwise noted, the author and the publisher make no explicit guarantees as to the accuracy of the information contained in this book and in some cases, names of people and places have been altered to protect their privacy.

Scripture quotations are from The Holy Bible, English Standard Version® (ESV®), copyright © 2001 by Crossway, a publishing ministry of Good News Publishers. Used by permission. All rights reserved.

Scripture quotations taken from the New American Standard Bible®, Copyright © 1960, 1962, 1963, 1968, 1971, 1972, 1973, 1975, 1977, 1995 by The Lockman Foundation. Used by permission. (www.Lockman.org)

Good News Translation® (Today's English Version, Second Edition) Copyright © 1992 American Bible Society. All rights reserved.

WestBow Press books may be ordered through booksellers or by contacting:

WestBow Press
A Division of Thomas Nelson & Zondervan
1663 Liberty Drive
Bloomington, IN 47403
www.westbowpress.com
1 (866) 928-1240

Because of the dynamic nature of the Internet, any web addresses or links contained in this book may have changed since publication and may no longer be valid. The views expressed in this work are solely those of the author and do not necessarily reflect the views of the publisher, and the publisher hereby disclaims any responsibility for them.

Any people depicted in stock imagery provided by Thinkstock are models, and such images are being used for illustrative purposes only. Certain stock imagery © Thinkstock.

ISBN: 978-1-5127-1653-5 (sc)
ISBN: 978-1-5127-1654-2 (hc)
ISBN: 978-1-5127-1652-8 (e)

Library of Congress Control Number: 2015917148

Print information available on the last page.

WestBow Press rev. date: 10/14/2015

Contents

Acknowledgments ix
Introduction xi

1. Re-imagine 1
2. A Palace and a Stable 3
3. Part of the Gift Is Responsibility 5
4. Mary's Maturity 7
5. Holding and Being Held 9
6. Joseph and Me 11
7. My Temple Existence 13
8. Obfuscate? Really? 14
9. Anticipation 16
10. Theo? 17
11. Blessing and Destiny 18
12. Healing in His Wings 20
13. Finding Creativity 22
14. Lessons from Doggy Breath 24
15. The "See-Through" Gospel 26
16. A Blown Prayer Fuse 28
17. I'm Adorable? 30
18. Terrorist Love 32
19. Generous Gratitude 34
20. Thank You for Reading This! 36
21. Tears to Joy 38
22. There's Only One Person I Want behind Me 40
23. In the Middle of This Madness 42
24. God's Kiss 44

25.	Promises to Keep	45
26.	Death's Promise	47
27.	What Was David Building?	49
28.	Fahgettaboudit!	50
29.	Just Wining	51
30.	Stronger than Dirt	53
31.	The Truth Came First	55
32.	The Condemned Sin	57
33.	My Real Name	59
34.	Two Priorities	61
35.	This Stuff Works!	63
36.	The Right Location	65
37.	A Toothless Hiss	66
38.	Caused and Covered	67
39.	I Want to Hold Your Hand	69
40.	Our Simeon Ancestry	70
41.	Unwrapping the Gift of Years	71
42.	Years Ago, This Was the Future	73
43.	A Positive Calendar	75
44.	Little Lamps, Shining Lights	77
45.	Influencing Bithia	79
46.	Pass? Stay?	81
47.	Good Advice from the Doc	83
48.	A Little Boy, a Boat, and a Father	85
49.	Coffee-Cup Guidance	87
50.	The Order of Things	88
51.	Run!	90
52.	Core Grace	91
53.	Future Realities Impact Present Ideologies	93
54.	God's Mark	95
55.	The Gift of Empty	97
56.	Still Rolls the Stone	98
57.	Details, Details, Details	99
58.	Challenging Cartoons	101
59.	What's in a Name?	103
60.	The Toothpaste Test	105

61.	Getting a Head Start(ed)	107
62.	Just Thinking	109
63.	Memorial Stones	111
64.	Psycho Pure	113
65.	Flowery Thoughts	115
66.	Thinking Habits	116
67.	Screening Thoughts	117
68.	Always Blooming	119
69.	Changed Stones	121
70.	Live Bread	122
71.	Small Hurt, Major Pain	123
72.	Nicknamed by Jesus	124
73.	Escaping to the Right Place	125
74.	Daily Transformation	127
75.	Victorious Secret	129
76.	My Own Little Sign	130
77.	The Dr. Seuss Conviction	131
78.	Longing for the Day	133
79.	Seed Power	134
80.	A Sunny Destination	136
81.	Check with the Author First	138
82.	Seeking Mission Wisdom	140
83.	Mowing Spirituality	142
84.	My Septic Perspective	144
85.	No More Lost Days	146
86.	Reflected Image	147
87.	Unseen Influence	149
88.	Childish Learning	150
89.	Planted Fruit	152
90.	An Awkward Situation	154
91.	The Hills Are Alive	156
92.	Blazing a Trail	158
93.	Seeking a Glimpse	159
94.	Easier with My Father	161
95.	A Watery Lesson	163
96.	A Daily Gift	164

97.	In the "Q"	166
98.	Amram's Legacy	167
99.	Credit to the Source	169
100.	One More Thing	171

About the Author 173

Acknowledgments

Life is a team effort. Like John Donne said, "No man is an island, entire of himself." Just being alive connects us to many others, more than we can imagine. There is nothing that is not a team effort. So when an author's name is placed on a book, it doesn't tell the whole story.

Many have been involved in the writing of this book. There is my supportive, cherished wife, Shirley; and my reassuring children, Annie Marie, Zac, and Zac's wife, Annie Michelle. My grandchildren (Hannah, Ben, and Sarah) also deserve credit. All of these make me feel as if my life is worthwhile, and they always love me, regardless of how I'm feeling. To them, this book is dedicated.

Then there is Kim Weurtz, friend first but also editor and publisher. Without her help, this would have been a collection of random thoughts printed on a blog that never left the computer.

There are countless others—friends, family, acquaintances—whose contributions to my life have altered how I see things. In fact, they did alter how I see things, and that's the point of my appreciation for them. As you read this, if you think you might be one of those people, then you probably are. Then there are the countless others I've observed but never met. You, who would be innocent bystanders, are also contributors without your knowing it. For through the observations, you've touched me.

But first of all there is my Father, to whose Book I have dedicated my life. I pray his words shape my thoughts and have the greatest influence. From him, I have learned the most important thing—to love.

Introduction

This book is largely a collection of thoughts and impressions. It comes from circumstances I have experienced, movies I have seen, recollection I have had, and from just about any source that tricks me into that which I sometimes avoid—thinking.

You may disagree with what you read. In fact, I might too when I read it. The idea isn't to give you unblemished instruction but rather to ignite your thinking and excite your own creativity when it comes to understanding and pursuing leadership. These are thoughts I've recorded, right or wrong—just thoughts. I must say without hesitation that they are good. You may disagree. I have had wonderful, eye-opening, beautiful, glorious, astonishing, innovative thoughts in the past with which others have disagreed. You won't be the first or the last.

Here is my desire: read and think. The chapters, if you can call them that, are very short. A couple of paragraphs are my usual attention span, and then I start to wander off in other directions. But they are also short so that they don't include too much information for your reaction. Space is left in the margins and between chapters so you can jot down your own notes, ideas, and observations. I hope that these words would cause you to think and evaluate and even lead you in some conclusions that are beneficial and helpful to you and others around you.

In the spaces provided, take notes. Gather your own ideas. Share them with others. Continue your spiritual experience and journey. Maybe sometime we'll have the opportunity to sit down and think out loud together. It would be great to learn from you.

So let's get started, and please—have fun!

1

Re-imagine

I came across this quote in Tom Peter's book, *Re-Imagine*: "But we must appreciate that design is the Seat of the Soul ... if one is in the Solutions-Experiences-Dream-Fulfillment Business."

That is the business I want to be in—the solutions-experiences-dream-fulfillment business. But what is that? How do I get there from here?

I guess maybe it is an attitude toward life. I mean, if you are in business or part of a business, then to think that way will overhaul that (your) business. But as a matter of personal habit, to look at life that way—what a thought!

I want to solve problems, not be one. Those of you who know me may not believe that, but maybe I'm growing up (or tired). I want to experience life, not just live it. (That sounds familiar.) I also want those who know me best to enjoy that experience as I enjoy the experience of not just knowing them but also experiencing them. I want to see dreams fulfilled—my own and those of everyone around me. I want life to be a constant source of amazement and wonder.

Jesus said he came to give life in all its fullness. I'm not sure I have bought into that completely, especially (or because) of the way it is usually preached. You know what I mean—the health-and-wealth mentality. Maybe Jesus saw me as a problem that needed solving, an experience that needed happening, and a dream that needed fulfilling. Maybe he's working on that in me. Maybe he wants me to demonstrate that for others.

The apostle Paul wrote in two of his letters that we should seize the moment and take advantage of every opportunity. I don't want to just be ready to do that; I want to do it. Queen Esther of Old Testament fame was told that maybe the reason she became queen was to handle the problem that had come to be. Maybe today, every day, I can be in the solutions-experiences-dream-fulfillment business.

Going back to the quote—"design is the seat of the soul." If it is going to happen, it is like everything significant that I have ever wanted that has happened. It will have to be by design and desire. Maybe I would change the quote: design and desire combine to form the seat of the soul.

2

A Palace and a Stable

I was thinking the other day about Herod and the palace he had built just a few miles southeast of Bethlehem. Apparently, it was quite a palace and resembled a volcano. It was well fortified, and the towers were such that a person (Herod) could go into one and be safe from attacking enemies. Herod the Great is said to be buried there, but excavations have not unearthed a body or tomb.

It was quite a structure, and being only about six (or fewer) miles from Bethlehem, it was probably visible from parts of the little town. And it is quite likely that the shepherds from Luke's gospel could easily have admired the structure from their sheep's grazing hillsides.

So here is a great palace fortress built by a crazy king, just a short distance from the stable where Christ was born.

I love paradox, and here's one: a crazy king who regularly exalted himself and angered the Jews built a palace just a short distance from the place where the real, everlasting King of the Jews would be born. Perhaps the shepherds were with their sheep between the Herodium and the manger. The angel—then angels—appeared and instructed them where to go. There in the distance was the great palace of the king, a tremendous structure and archeological accomplishment. But they were instructed to go to Bethlehem and look for a baby wrapped in rags and lying in a feeding trough.

The shepherds came to Bethlehem and found the newborn King, and his name was Jesus! Proverbs 18:10 says that the name of the Lord is a strong tower where the righteous can go and be safe. It isn't just the baby; it's the meaning of his name—a promise from God that Jehovah is salvation.

A crazed, paranoid lunatic built a tower, thinking he could be safe there, and a few miles away, maybe in the tower's shadow, a grand plan unfolded, as well as a simple object lesson to teach us that real safety—eternal security—is a (Christmas) gift from God.

3

Part of the Gift Is Responsibility

I remember a special Christmas when I received a BB gun. I hadn't had it very long before I shot a window in Grandma's house. It was a back-porch window, and the gun only made a little hole. Grandma wasn't too bothered by it, but my dad ... I was banished to the woods for any other displays of marksmanship.

Not too far from a creek, I found some old bottles and practiced shooting them. I was steadily improving when our dog, Prince, went to investigate my prowess a little closer. He cut his foot rather badly on a shard from a bottle I had hit. This time, my dad was afraid to tell my mother, and I was banished a little deeper into the woods.

Okay, glass was no longer a target. But a passing bird caught my attention. The tiny fellow lit a little closer than advisable, and I made a shot Davy Crockett would have been proud of. The bird dropped like a lead weight, and I was smiling with glee and bursting at the seams. My favorite aunt, Jean, happened to be traveling to Grandma's, and I stopped her on the road to display my bagged game. I knew she would be delighted and proud and would probably take me to town for some Dairy Queen ice cream. Well, I've never seen her mad before or since. She said it was terrible, as well as illegal, to shoot a bluebird—the state bird. I promised her a lesson learned, and neither Mom nor Dad nor Grandma had to know.

So you may think this is about Red Ryder BB guns, putting an eye out, or acting responsibly. Sort of—it is about getting what you want but not handling it responsibly. We celebrate Christmas as the birth of the Savior and rightly so. But it comes with great responsibility. We have gotten not only what we wanted, but also the only thing we really needed.

Maybe I should give this a think: to celebrate Christmas is to take responsibility to live a life that measures up to the standard of having a Savior. The gift of Christmas is the possibility of salvation, and grace is the condition we live under when we receive it.

I hope to have the best Christmas ever, and maybe someone around me can have his or her best Christmas ever because of something I do or say. Maybe you can make this true for you and someone around you too!

4

Mary's Maturity

What does it mean to treasure up things in your heart? I have some great memories that I hold very close. I often think about them when traveling, alone, or in contemplative moods:

- Shirley's and my first kiss
- my son's birth
- my daughter and I in front of our first fireplace
- my first granddaughter's bedtime kiss
- taking my grandson to the sport show
- my second granddaughter learning to crawl and then coming to me
- my daughter-in-law's first quilt

I have lots of them, and all are surrounded by great times with the people I love the most.

But in the Christmas story in Luke, we read that after the shepherds' visit to the manger, Mary treasured things in her heart and pondered them.

An angel appeared and said, "You're going to be pregnant and deliver the Son of God." After that, nothing seemed to go right. An unplanned and unexplainable pregnancy, a shotgun wedding, an unplanned trip to be enrolled in a census, a manger for a crib, animals for attendants, unknown shepherds (not family) coming to visit, magi bringing gifts, the innocent slaughter of children, a move to Egypt—all that we know and even more we can speculate. All in all, considering that she carried and delivered the Son of God, we might have expected things to be much easier for her.

So she treasured up and pondered. At first she asked, "Why me?" But afterward, she accepted that she was the Lord's handmaid, whatever he said was fine, and she would handle it with him. But did she have any idea what would happen? Still, she treasured and pondered.

Did I think becoming a Christian would make everything easy? Do I expect preferential treatment? In becoming a Christian, wasn't I saying, "Behold, I am a servant of the Lord; let it be to me according to your word"?

The gift of Jesus is the best gift and the only gift I have ever really needed. May his life (and Mary's) teach me to treasure up the difficult, questionable, doubt-filled, and fearful moments in my life and lead me to ponder them, understanding these are treasures of the magnificent plan of God to bring me to maturity. It isn't in the good times or the great memories but in the opposite that my Christianity makes a statement.

This Christmas will indeed give me treasurable experiences. May one of them be to learn that I must truly treasure every situation (each and every one) as God's continual work in me.

5

Holding and Being Held

We spent Christmas at my sister and brother-in-law's cabin. It has become our family tradition. It is such a great time that I always want the last thing we do before leaving to be praying together. But I am much too emotional. It takes the fifteen miles back to St. James for me to be able to talk without my voice cracking. To try to pray together would be embarrassing. I pray silently.

This year, I spent a lot of time holding eight-month-old Sarah. I loved every minute. Even when others would give out funny noises and make faces when she spit up on me, I didn't mind. Holding her reminded me of holding Ben and Hannah, my other grandchildren, when they were small. And then came memories of holding Zac and Annie, my children, when they were small. And it all started with the grandest of holdings on July 6, 1972, when Shirley and I decided to start dating. I cherish that memory most fondly.

I wonder what my folks and grandparents felt when they held me as a small child. There are many people I miss this time of year. Embracing the thoughts of the coming kingdom of God is my hope and security. But it would be nice to be held by my mom and grandparents one more time. I find myself hugging my father longer these days.

What did people experience when they held the infant Jesus? We know a little about Simeon and Anna, but what about the shepherds and the magi? What about Elizabeth and Zechariah, John the Baptist's parents? They had some special insight about Jesus because of their relationship with Mary and the circumstances of John's birth. After the angelic revelations they experienced, how did Mary and Joseph do anything but hold him—physically and in awe?

But my question today is this: how did the grandparents hold him? I have no clue, but from a grandparent's perspective, I truly wonder. Right now, I am thinking that one of the attributes of love that makes it the greatest is the ability it gives to hold and be held.

When Jesus returns, I look forward to holding and being held. I have a lot I want to hold and a lot by which I want to be held, including Jesus on both counts. It's a good thing forever's forever.

6

Joseph and Me

I'm having a hard time moving on from Christmas. The holiday is a favorite time of the year, and the Christmas story is so fascinating. Today I was thinking about Joseph. The story surrounding him is pretty short and simple, but what we can speculate can go on forever—correct or incorrect.

One of the things I surmise is that as Mary was chosen so was Joseph. In other words, it wasn't that Mary was chosen to be the mother of Jesus, and Joseph just happened to be engaged to her but rather that Mary and Joseph were chosen to be the parents. As Mary had found favor with the Lord, so had Joseph. Just as Mary had met whatever requirements were necessary and had somehow lived up to the qualifications, so had Joseph. And some would argue that it was all grace and not necessarily Mary's or Joseph's character, but even so, Joseph is a key player and was woven into the fabric of the story.

When we look at the little we know about him, we see only good—a just man not wanting to humiliate Mary for her "condition." But when we look at his situation, we see a lot of stress—not only marrying a pregnant woman; not only the census, the flight to Egypt, the return to Nazareth to avoid Archelaus but the untold story of his life and death during the life of Jesus.

Craig Wagganer

Too often, I think it should be easy. I mean, shouldn't Mary and Joseph have had it easy, considering their circumstances and being the parents of the Son of God? That's my feeling. But of course I say this wanting the same thing for myself. If I do good, shouldn't God make life easy for me? I want to be obedient and get rewarded for it now. Even saying this reveals my immaturity and selfishness, which disqualifies me—oh, the paradox.

So here it is, from Joseph ...

Mary and Joseph grew into their relationship of trust with God; they didn't just arrive there.

There was a certain glory in the relationship they had with God and that brought them to the position of parenthood.

They were not protected from the stress of the experience.

The last is the problem. I want to grow to be like Joseph in my character, but I want the circumstances to be different. It is clear I am not finished growing yet.

7

My Temple Existence

So Jesus went into the temple and saw it being abused in a way that burned his fuse all the way into the core. He blew up. The temple was to be a house of prayer, but it had been turned into a place of business—and dirty business at that.

Maybe what I need to understand about the temple that I am is that I am to be a house of God's communication. I am a dwelling for his divine correspondence with me—and me with him. But I am also the place where his communication with those he has not yet been able to inhabit takes place. (You may have to read these sentences a few times for them to make sense. Sorry. And my apologies to those proficient in English who know how I should have said all that.)

I am a house of prayer; he and I in union, He and the world in touch. He in me, and me in them. That sounds kind of familiar.

The next time my phone rings I'll be reminded of this. There are times when God and I talk together in this temple. But there are times when God talks to me, and I need to—have to—tell the world, "It's for you."

8

Obfuscate? Really?

Obfuscate.

I came across that word while reading. *What?*

So I checked an online dictionary. Here you go, in case you didn't know: obfuscate—to make so confused or opaque as to be difficult to perceive or understand.

I laughed; the word itself was obfuscating. I thought about the word and the phrase you hear people say sometimes: "That really muddied the water."

We really do muddy the water. I mean, we really obfuscate. We're experts at it and didn't even know it. I wonder, if I told someone I could be a professional obfuscatician (you'll have to practice saying that; I've been working on it about ten minutes so far), if he or she would understand. (Get it?) I wonder how I would apply. I suppose I already have; I just don't get paid for it. (Now that's a confession!)

In business, in life, we have a need for clear water. Maybe that was what Jesus was saying when he offered living water. There was a lot of obfuscation around—some concerning religious life, some concerning the treacherous times, some concerning the living of life (like the woman at the well), and some about Jesus himself. I'm pretty sure there were others.

What I need to commit to for every area of life is living water. To make it a point to get rid of the obfuscation and make sure I am living clean, pure, holy. Yeah, every area. In every dealing, in every situation, in every circumstance, in every conversation, in every ... am I living water?

9

Anticipation

I came across a quote today, and I didn't write it down! Now, I know I am smarter than that. Or ... well ... I guess I'm not!

Anyway, it was from *Winnie-the-Pooh* and was something like, "The best feeling in the world is eating honey. No, it's the feeling you get right before you eat the honey."

Carly Simon did a song a long time ago, "Anticipation." And one of the key lines was "Anticipation is making me wait."

Isn't anticipation a great thing? The feeling of anticipation almost always elevates the culmination of the event. It kind of changes the meaning of "What are you waiting for?"

I think that is why Romans 4 tells us that Abraham grew stronger in faith the longer God's promise of a son didn't come true. He knew the promise would come true; he anticipated it. So each day was not a day it didn't happen but rather a day closer to the day it *would* happen.

I have had people ask me what it means to seek God's kingdom first. Maybe it has to do with anticipation. "What are you waiting for?"

Come, Lord Jesus, come.

10

Theo?

I thought about a statement I made a couple of times recently. I told several people, "I am not a theologian. I really don't know much theology and don't enjoy debating it." I'll admit I do enjoy a nice word rumble once in a while, but the older I get, the less I like a verbal tête-à-tête.

So I thought about the people I know and words like theology. Here is what I am coming to: a search for words to describe my situation, my thinking. I guess I'll make up a couple. "Theology" is fine— the study of God. But that really isn't where I am. I thought about "theography," but "graphy" means to describe or give characteristics. Sounds kind of like what you do after you've done the study. So I think I am into "theoscience." That would be the knowledge of God. I don't want to study or describe God as much as I really want to know him. Maybe that takes the other two, but it also takes an experience with him. That's my aim in every situation: to experience him.

I have a lot of acquaintances. I know about them; I can even describe them. I know other intimate friends and can tell you about them from my experience. I want my story concerning God, my testimony, not to be just description from study but from the experience I have of knowing him.

Ology? Graphy? Science? What's the right suffix for experiencing?

11

Blessing and Destiny

Last Sunday, taking communion in church had me thinking. It took me back to some research I had all but forgotten. It had to do with some of the symbolism of what Jesus did the night he was betrayed.

To share bread with someone was to share blessings. In other words, traditionally when you asked someone to share bread with you, you were making a statement that you had been blessed and wanted to share that part of God's goodness with the person you were inviting.

To share a cup with someone was to share destiny. That is, if I offer you to drink from the same cup from which I am drinking, I am inviting you to share my destiny. That could be good or bad.

So during the communion meal, Jesus took the bread of blessing and shared it with his followers. He then also took the cup of destiny and shared it with his followers. He gave them the blessing of redemption and the destiny of the kingdom.

Isn't that what we are now to share with those around us? The blessing of our redemption and the destiny of the coming kingdom of God. From now on when I take communion, it will not only be a memory tool to remember Christ until he comes but also a challenge to do what he taught me, using just a piece of unleavened bread and a little cup; share.

Two words I'll never think of the same way again: blessing and destiny.

12

Healing in His Wings

We have an interesting arrangement hanging on our living room wall. There is a *tallit* hanging next to a picture of Simeon holding Jesus (from Luke 2). I love the tallit and the picture; I can look at them and contemplate for long periods of time.

A tallit is a prayer shawl used by Jewish rabbis. It is longer than it is wide and is worn draped over the shoulders. When it is time to pray the shawl is lifted and used as a covering for the head. On the corners of the tallit are *tzitzits*. These are strings that hang down and are tied in five knots. The five knots are to remind the praying person of the five books of the Law of Moses, and the four spaces between the knots are to represent the four letters, or consonants, in God's name (YHWH).

Perhaps you know the story of the woman who had a terrible ailment that had something to do with bleeding. Her story is recorded in Matthew 9, as well as in Mark 5 and Luke 8. The story is that the woman was convinced that if she could just touch the hem of Jesus's garment, she would be healed. And she was right!

She touched the hem, but the word translated as hem—you guessed it—was tzitzit. Maybe she didn't just touch the bottom of his robe but rather one of the special cords that hung in five knots from the corner of his prayer shawl. This would take little more effort than just grabbing at the bottom of his robe. Maybe it explains why others may have been crowding and touching him, but she was healed.

But really, what difference does it make? I'm not sure it makes any difference, but I remember wearing the tallit while speaking once. At one point, I draped it over my shoulders and took the edges of the garment in my hands and held them up. Afterward, I was told that I looked like I had angel wings!

Isn't there a prophecy in Malachi and in Ezekiel or somewhere that indicates that Messiah will come with healing in his wings? I wonder if this woman, sensing and experiencing Jesus as Messiah, had faith to touch his wings, claim the prophecy, and was healed. I wonder what wings that gave her.

13

Finding Creativity

I was working on an upcoming class and needed some ideas. I turned to my first line of resources. When it comes to needing a spark of creativity, I readily acknowledge my two trusted resources.

One resource is my *Calvin and Hobbes* books; I have many. I spin my chair around, choose a book, and begin to read about the little character's escapades. Mr. Watterson, the cartoonist who created the comic strip, has a great imagination and a creativity that helps me get moving. I may spend a little too much reading and rereading, but I always come away with an improved attitude and great ideas—and some of them are useful.

The other resource for challenging me to be more creative is the Bible. I have several Bibles as well, and I can begin reading and thinking about situations, and I always find a spark of creativity from the insights.

One of the first things we learn about God is that he is creative. In the beginning, he demonstrated his creativity. Of course, there are myriad examples, but I love taking the grandkids to the zoo, because even an elementary look at the animal kingdom reveals just the tip of God's infinite creativity.

I suppose as I face problems—situations in my life in which I beg his intervention; circumstances in which I feel powerless or need his power—it is comforting to know that he is creative. And I have seen it demonstrated in those areas of my life.

God's creativity is seen all around in nature, but when we look at his activity in our own lives, we see that he is very creative there as well. As I face those circumstances in which I ask for him to work, he always does and usually in a way I wasn't expecting. I pray and set up conditions and expectations as a result of the need I see, the pressure I feel, and the outcome I desire and/or expect. But when all is resolved I find that God has worked in a completely different and much better way. He has been creative.

Perhaps trust and faith are about realizing the creativity of God to work in a situation in which every tangent situation (known and unknown) is reconciled to him and by him. He continues his creativity in having everything under control and working all things together for good, according to his purpose, not just for me but for everyone involved and in the grand scheme of his coming kingdom.

Maybe an integral part of my prayers should be for me to see, comprehend, and be challenged by his creativity, that I will continue to be amazed and be in awe.

14

Lessons from Doggy Breath

We're babysitting our son's family dog this weekend. He is a yellow Lab named Henry. He is a great dog, minds well, doesn't bark much, and is no trouble. I think he knows his name, but I am not sure. You see, he often gets called by the name of previous dogs in the family. Sometimes he's Indeo, other times KC, and sometimes he even gets called by the names of the children in the family. I suppose if someone heard me call him, they might think his full name is "Hannah-Ben-Sarah-Henry!"

He is a beautiful dog and a great family pet. He is great with the kids, and I am sure that there was nothing on the application for family dog that cautioned him about the eight- and five-year-olds, as well as the eleven-month-old. When he came, there were only two kids. I don't think anybody asked him about options or his opinion on a third.

The Bible says in Ecclesiastes 3:19 that man and animals all have the same breath. We live; we die; that's the story of each. But when I am around Henry—petting, playing, or just in the same room—his breath is pretty bad. I know that "breath" in the biblical sense has a different meaning than what I have mentioned, but it does make me wonder.

Is the breath of my life a pleasing aroma to God? When I open my mouth to him, is it "minty fresh" or dog offensive? I know what I want, what I strive for, but it isn't my desire that matters; it is what delights God. I can think of all kinds of ways to improve my life for him, but the mandate is to check what he wants and hen provide it. Learn to desire what he does, not what I think.

So man does not live by bread alone but by every word from the mouth of God. That's what I want—his breath to be my breath. Every time he breathes out, I breathe in. When he speaks a word, I take it in. I read once that it is no more awesome to hear the voice of God than to read his Word. Ah, the awesomeness of the breath I feel when I open his Word.

15

The "See-Through" Gospel

I was wondering about the effectiveness of Christians. Seems like if we were more joyful in our dispositions and more loving in our actions, then the world would be much more interested in listening to us, and our message would be much more successful.

In Numbers 33, it says that "on the day after Passover the people of Israel went out triumphantly." Easter—I prefer "Resurrection Sunday"—is our Passover. As a result of the resurrection of Jesus, we have been delivered from death to life. We should be going out triumphantly. It should be easy to tell the people of the resurrection. We should be different from everyone else. Jesus's triumph is ours and that makes all the difference.

When the people of Israel left Egypt, they wound up in the wilderness, and we all know the problems they faced and the destruction they caused. They lived between the promise and the fulfillment. That's where we are. Through the resurrection of Jesus, God has promised that there is a kingdom coming, and we are the inheritors. The promise has been made; we are waiting for the promise to be fulfilled.

The people of Israel left Egypt with a promise of a land of their own. But the trip there was difficult. God had made a promise; the people were to trust him. They had been released from slavery and were headed to the Promised Land. But along the way they got distracted from the promise by their own selfishness.

We live between the promise and the fulfillment. We are in the wilderness. Are we trusting the promise or selfishly looking at our circumstances? We have been given a promise, and the deliverance is a sure thing, but do we live like it?

Hebrews 12 says that Jesus endured the cross because of the joy set before him. He could see past the suffering to the resurrection. The cross had a window in the middle. The pain and suffering were there, but no one could take away the joy that would come. He had "see-through" good news. He gave us a "see-through" gospel.

While in the wilderness, I need to concentrate on the see-through gospel. The wilderness is not the kingdom, but I am heading to the kingdom. This wilderness is the time for me to go out "triumphantly," seeing through this life to the promise of the kingdom.

Anticipation is what the see-through gospel is all about. Speaking of Jesus, Hebrews says, "Who for the joy set before him ..." May I always see the joy set before me.

May God richly bless your Resurrection Sunday.

16

A Blown Prayer Fuse

Our washing machine went out. It ran through all the cycles; it was just that the motor didn't appear to do its job. I could hear clicking and noises that made me think the electronics were working fine, but somehow the motor wasn't getting the signal.

I took the front off the machine. I gazed at it for a while. Got down on the ground and pushed and pulled wires. Thumped a few things; gave the motor a good knock. Started it all up again but without any improvement. I repeated my previous actions but with a little more authority. Still no response. To me, it seemed like it must be the motor, so I looked for a reset button but found none. I pushed and pulled all the wires connected to the motor. I gave it a good slap on the side—still nothing.

This washer is much more complicated, with all the electronics, than the older ones. This one is just a few years old and looks simple, but everything has become more electronic. There isn't a lot to take apart and look for problems, and problems are not as evident. So after my ineffective tries, I called a repairman, expecting to have to replace the motor. Once that was determined, I was sure I could replace the motor myself.

Rick showed up and began his own diagnostics. He used a meter and checked the electrical current on several things and then mentioned it could be a fuse in the wiring. He used a knife and wire cutter to expose a little electronic fuse about the size of a grape nut. Sure enough, that was the problem; he replaced it and was on his way to his next call.

I looked at that little fuse. Something so small that kept the whole machine from working.

Psalm 66:18 says, "If my thoughts had been sinful, he would have refused to hear me." Oftentimes I am tempted to become impatient with God in answering my prayers. Perhaps I need to look for something small in my life that may be interfering with the relationship. Maybe there is a small, insignificant part of my life (from my perspective) that I haven't revealed to him that is hindering the relationship.

I looked at that tiny little fuse and thought, *There are some big lessons in this!*

17

I'm Adorable?

Last evening was my grandson's first baseball game. Well, it was kind of like baseball. They used a pitching machine, and each child received five pitches to hit the ball. If, after the five pitches, the child hadn't made a hit, a tee was brought out and the child got to hit off the tee.

So every child got a hit, which means every person's batted ball had to be played by the defense. So here is a ground ball hit to the right side (or left side or up the middle) of the infield. First the fielders all stare at the ball until the voices of the coaches and parents are heard screaming, "Go get it!" At that point the ball is deluged by four- and five-year-olds. I am glad, for the ball's sake, that it is an inanimate object; the attack would be too much for a living thing to endure.

Once the ball is retrieved by one, then a decision has to be made on what to do with it. Now you have the rest of the team yelling, "Throw it," each voice giving his or her opinion as to the direction. In the confusion, the child chooses a target and lets loose. Now the outfield gets to chase down the sphere. And this continues until a coach has finally retrieved the ball and is ready to pitch to the next batter.

The outs, when they happen (rarely), are not counted. The runs scored (often) are not counted. Every player on each team bats in his or her offensive inning. Defensively, the players are put into position, which lasts as long as a coach is watching; then the social nature of each individual comes out as the child moves around to be closer to friends, to share seeing an airplane or bug, or maybe to run to parents or grandparents to make a trip to the bathroom or whatever distraction calls. The game is not played by innings but by time. The game is limited to an hour, so the next set of children and parents can enjoy the introduction of the national pastime to another generation.

It is quite a sight. I have attended many professional baseball games and don't ever recall the word "cute" being used, but that was the most-often-heard phrase at the field last evening. And it was more than just correct. They were absolutely adorable.

At the top of the list of absolutely adorable was my grandson, Ben, in his blue and red uniform. But I also got to hold my almost one-year-old granddaughter, Sarah, during most of the game, while while enjoying the clever, witty, and absolutely hilarious conversations with my eight-year-old Hannah. These three topped the list. But I was also aware that as many children as there were taking part, there were family members watching, feeling the same pride for their own as I was feeling for mine.

Matthew 19:14 says, "Jesus said, 'Let the little children come to me and do not hinder them, for to such belongs the kingdom of heaven.'" Holding Sarah, watching Ben, listening to Hannah ... God loves them so very dearly. But looking at the field, he loves every one of them. And then looking at the people around the field—they are God's children. Jesus welcomes them as family. He even loves me. I was overwhelmed.

18

Terrorist Love

Almost two weeks ago, bombs exploded at the Boston Marathon. A week ago, one of those responsible was killed and another taken into custody. I have heard the outcry against these two young men and what they represent. It makes me very, very sad.

It is obvious that someone talked to them about Islam. In fact, someone went beyond that and influenced them into some radical form of hatred. As I read and pray and weep, I wonder ...

The language thrown about is that radical Islam leads to hatred and heinous crimes against humanity. I don't know if that is the truth or not. But what I understand from reading my Bible is that radical Christianity is the unwavering display of love in every situation. Christians attacked should be the exact opposite of hate groups that retaliate with more hatred. As Christians, our radical nature should be to love. And the worse the crime, the deeper our love; the greater the offense, the greater our compassion.

Christians crying out for justice? Are we not the very ones who praise the Lord for forgiveness and speak of receiving mercy? Aren't we taught that to receive mercy we must extend mercy; to be forgiven, forgive?

We show pictures of the terrorists standing alongside the child who became a victim of his crime, and we are mad instead of sad. In the next instant, we look upon our Savior hanging on a cross for us and speak of love. We see the terrorists and their victim, and we hate. I wonder what Jesus felt, looking down from the cross and seeing each of us that put him there. Actually, there is evidence of what he felt, and it is to be my paradigm.

Someone talked to the two young men about Islam. I wonder if anyone (any one of us) talked to them about Jesus. As sad as radical hate groups are that take a pinch of religion and exaggerate it into something deadly, much more sad is Christianity that is comfortable with retaliation and cries for justice.

If it is true (and I am not saying it is; I don't know) that radical Islam leads to terrorism, why is it that Christianity has become so cold as to not love as Jesus loved?

Lord, protect me from becoming comfortable with human understanding and wisdom. Give me wisdom from above to forgive as I have been forgiven, to be compassionate as I have received compassion, to love as I have been loved, to offer hope as I have received hope, and to speak as I have been spoken to.

19

Generous Gratitude

This week I led a presentation for a local Chamber of Commerce. The subject matter was showing sincere appreciation for people. It included a time of recognizing the strengths and contributions of others and showing appreciation by doing a little more than just saying thanks.

The next day I spent the morning and early afternoon as a "parent helper" for my grandson's preschool, after which we enjoyed a treat and then went home to play basketball. When the time came, I walked up to my granddaughter's school and met her at the front door. We walked home; she did her homework, and then she and I went to see Gram's (that's what they call my wife, their grandmother) new office. After touring the office, we went out to eat, played games while waiting for our order, ate pizza, and then it was time to head home.

On the way back to the house, my granddaughter found a blank piece of paper and announced she was going to do an acrostic poem. She worked hard, folded the paper, and put it in my pocket. Later, I took the paper out of my pocket and read it (in her words and spelling) ...

> Toatolly cool
> Happy
> Always nice
> Never mean

      Kind
      Yippy
      On top of the world
      Unmean
      To: Pop
      From: Hannah W.

In many of the apostle Paul's writings, he mentions being thankful for people. I learn so much from my grandchildren. I had taught a class on showing appreciation, and then I received one of the nicest gestures I have ever received, something I'll treasure forever.

Never underestimate the power of generous gratitude. I am now thanking God for everyone who takes time from their busy schedules to read my thoughts. Thank you so very much, and God's blessings on you.

20

Thank You for Reading This!

I did a program last week for a local Covenant House. I have been familiar with this organization since the late 1970s and know they do a tremendous service to their communities by helping teens who may be displaced or homeless. They do fantastic work—a lot more than providing housing. They work hard to help the young people become productive members of society. They demonstrate love and caring in very practical ways.

As I mentioned, I did a program for them. It was a short presentation on showing appreciation, followed by a scavenger hunt at the St. Louis Zoo. It was a blast. These are fantastic people with a lot of energy, creativity, and even a bit of a competitive spirit. They participated well, and the pictures and videos they took during the scavenger hunt were very entertaining.

But the one thing that stood out was that in the mail a few days afterward, I received a group picture; taken at the event, with the names of the participants, along with some short messages. I was thrilled to receive such a gift and have it proudly displayed in our living room. It will eventually move to my office, but not before I have shared it with as many people as possible.

It was a joy and is now a treasured memory to interact with these wonderful people. I enjoyed being with them and learning from them as much as making the presentation for them. But it really burned in my mind the importance of showing appreciation. What they did gave me such a wonderful feeling. It is so nice to be appreciated. We talked about it at the event, and their demonstration brought it home.

In 1 Chronicles 16:8 it says, "Oh give thanks to the Lord; call upon his name; make known his deeds among the peoples!" Certainly, we give thanks to God for what he has done, is doing, and will do. Shouldn't that teach me to be thankful to others as well? Showing appreciation is a much-needed characteristic that marks a person of integrity and gratitude.

Lord help me to say thank you to whom it is due and even beyond that. May I be marked as a person of generous gratitude—to you and those around me. Amen.

21

Tears to Joy

It made me cry. I have a coffee cup that my granddaughter Hannah made me for my birthday two years ago. It has red, green, and blue vertical stripes and reads "Pop" in big black letters. I was talking with my daughter about a week ago and told her that this cup is one of my absolute favorite things. Today, reaching for a cup, I picked up one and then saw Hannah's gift. I set the first cup down and picked up my favorite. As I headed for the coffeepot, I dropped it. I couldn't believe it; I just stared and started to cry. I had lost something so meaningful; I had dropped it and broke it.

I had reached for another cup; why did I change cups? I would not have minded dropping the first one. It was a cup with some special meaning, but I certainly would have rather lost it than the one Hannah made for me. How frustrating! How could I be so careless with something so valuable to me?

So here is the plan: I am going to make an appointment with Hannah and with Ben and Sarah. We'll go to the Painted Zebra shop, and I'll have them each make me a new coffee mug. Hannah is eight, Ben is five, and Sarah is one. It should be an adventure. I am getting excited about the plan. Now I'll have three keepsakes instead of just the one.

In Genesis, Joseph goes through a lot of trouble, but in the end, he realizes, by faith, that what may be intended for bad, God uses for good. In the New Testament book of Ephesians, Paul writes, concerning our adversary, that we should be able to stand against his schemes. In Romans, he says that all things work together for good to those who love the Lord.

I cried over my loss, but in a simple way, God taught me a great lesson that applies on a much larger scale. We never lose an object; rather, we gain an experience (and perhaps learn a lesson). The memory of Hannah's original gift will never be forgotten. No one, no thing, and no enemy can destroy that. But the experience has caused me to add an adventure with the grandchildren that will become dearer to me than the mugs they make.

I regret and am sorry that I broke the coffee mug, but I am grateful God healed my heart.

22

There's Only One Person I Want behind Me

I just returned from a trip to Sam's Club. About once a month, we go to stock up on a few things we feel are a good buy. Today, I had some extra time and decided I would get it out of the way and go by myself.

Big mistake.

I accomplished the task, but my partner wasn't there. I couldn't ask her questions, so there was no one to provide me with suitable answers. I felt very insecure in some of the items I purchased.

I kept second-guessing myself and really didn't think too much about it—until I saw myself in an aisle mirror. Then I smiled, because I am sure I provided some entertainment to other shoppers as they watched me pick up one thing after another, put something back and replace it with something else, and then two aisles later run back to make another exchange.

With a full cart, I was almost to the checkout lane when I realized I didn't have the mixed nuts. There are many items I would not have gone back for, but I can't go without the mixed nuts. Out of the line and back to find the nuts. I am sure people were observing, and if they'd known what I was going after, they would have said I had eaten too many nuts, and they've gone to my head. With nuts in the cart, I headed back to the checkout.

When you're not used to doing something by yourself, it can be pressing—at least for me it's pressing to do it on my own. Maybe I'm insecure or get lonely making decisions by myself. Maybe I count on my partner to help more than I should, but I don't think so; I just really need her.

I am glad that the trip to Sam's isn't a metaphor for life—or maybe it is. In things that matter, in seeking the kingdom first, there is a promised voice behind me, whispering, protecting, and advocating a certain way to go (Isaiah 20:31).

23

In the Middle of This Madness

A robin just landed on a power line outside my office window. It was singing up a storm. It caught my attention, and I watched it for as long as it stayed on the wire—just a few moments.

There were two things that caught my attention. One was the singing. This little bird was singing its heart out. My windows were closed; the air conditioner was going; there was some ambient background noise; and the music from the bird was still enough to capture my attention.

The second thing was that the wire was moving around from the weight of the bird's having landed on it. The wire bounced around, and the bird remained balanced and singing its song. It was a joy to watch and to listen.

The bird wasn't perched long before it spread its wings, made a push, and flew off into the air. But I remained, thinking about what I had seen in an instant.

I want to be like the bird on the wire. I want to be on top of any turbulence, troubling times, difficult circumstances, or problem situations. I want to be on top, singing.

I read recently—and I am trying to make it my personal philosophy—that it isn't how you weather the storm; it's learning to dance in the rain.

I think Bible-book author James may have been thinking this when he wrote, "Count it all joy when you meet trials of various kinds ..." And he followed it up with how the process works.

Today I am going to dance and sing. Others may see—or need to see—my joy.

24

God's Kiss

Last evening, Shirley and I went to our grandchildren's (Hannah, eight; Ben, five) last swim lesson of the summer. They have come a long way in the past couple of months, and it was fun and exciting to see their fear of the water turn into excitement. It was fun to see their enjoyment and to catch a glimpse of them looking over to see if we were watching.

But the best part was the end of the evening as we were saying goodbye. I had the honor of carrying baby Sarah to the car. As we walked, I talked with her. Her response, with her plugger in, was to lean and touch the plugger against me. She was giving me a kiss.

As I placed her in her car seat, Ben and Hannah busily got settled in and latched their seatbelts. I kissed each one; Sarah, plugger still in, threw me a kiss. Hannah and Ben both said they loved me. I gave them big, "I love you and am so proud of you!"

God must take tremendous pleasure in his grandchildren. That may sound funny, and I know we are all his children, but when a person is led to the Lord and then leads another generation to the Lord, which in turn leads another generation to the Lord ... that must really bring him pleasure.

I guess that is exactly why Jesus prayed for you and me in John 17:20 and for all those who *will* believe.

25

Promises to Keep

The St. Louis Zoo is really fantastic. It is one of the best zoos in the country, and they have some wonderful aspects that make it even better.

One great thing about the zoo is that it is free. Some attractions have a fee, but entrance to the zoo itself is free. Then there are several attractions that are free if you get there early. Here are some examples:

- Parking is free on the zoo lots before 8:15. (There is free parking throughout Forest Park, but it could be a walk to get to the zoo.)
- The cove where you can pet stingrays is free until 10:00 a.m.
- There is a great carousel for the kids that is free until 10:00 a.m.
- Even the children's zoo is free until 10:00 a.m.

So am I trying to drum up business for the St. Louis Zoo? No, it is a great attraction, but I bring it up because the zoo made me say something to my grandchildren that I am going to have to make good on.

Last week, I took them to a playground. We played for a while and then headed back to the house. I mentioned that I hadn't taken them to the zoo this year, and they began to get excited. Zoo talk is very stimulating to eight- and five-year-olds.

I mentioned this idea: "Why don't I come over one evening and we put up a tent in the backyard, camp out, and then go to the zoo early enough to take advantage of all the free stuff?"

They liked it.

Driving home, I began to have second thoughts on my ability to pull this off. My mouth thinks I am younger than I am. Then I came across this verse in Proverbs 12:15. "The way of a fool is right in his own eyes, but a wise man listens to advice."

Why didn't I ask for advice first? Oh well, at least I haven't set a date.

26

Death's Promise

I was asked to officiate at the funeral of a friend this week.

He was a great man. A wonderful family; a long, prestigious career; an impact on his community; a longtime faithful church member and tremendous supporter of that church. It was a pretty easy funeral, for the memories surrounding him were all positive, and even his future is sure because of his faith and the grace of God.

As I was preparing my comments, I came across a verse I was aware of but had not thought about for a long time. It's from Psalm 116 and simply states that the death of a saint is precious in the sight of God.

We rejoice at the birth of a child, and rightly so, for it is a time of rejoicing and celebration as we welcome the miracle of new life into our midst. But we realize that it can be a time of fear as well. We don't know what the journey of life holds for this child. We anticipate and pray for many joys and great and wonderful things ahead, but we also know of the many dangers that this life holds.

Perhaps the preciousness of the death of God's saints is that, now, one has made it safely to his or her rest. We were able to celebrate the life that had passed because this man had weathered every storm, with his Christian integrity firm. He was saved by the grace of God and never turned away from it. So he entered into this "nap" time in the sure hope of the resurrection, when Jesus returns. All who knew him knew of this hope of his, and his family and those of us friends who remain were able to celebrate his life looking forward, not back.

Surely death is a time of mourning, for we have lost someone who has given us something great. But how great it is to see joy through the tears and rejoice in the safety of rest and the anticipation of "Well done."

27

What Was David Building?

A couple of years ago, my wife and I received two Adirondack chairs. They weren't expensive but would make a nice addition to our backyard. Since the wood was soft pine, we decided they needed to be disassembled, primed, and painted. So with good intentions, we took them apart and bought the necessary paint and supplies.

This week we got the pieces out and painted them. The problem was putting them back together. Each chair had about thirty parts, along with myriad screws in three different sizes and quite a few bolts, washers, and nuts that also came in different sizes. How do the chairs go together? Which screws and bolts go where?

I downloaded a picture from the Internet that closely resembled our chairs and was able to complete assembly of both chairs in about three hours. I didn't mind the challenge, and I kind of enjoy puzzles. I conquered.

In Proverbs 3, it says that God created the world with wisdom, understanding, and knowledge. It is a tremendously humbling revelation to be stumped for a while by a thirty-piece puzzle and then consider the wisdom, understanding, and knowledge of God to create each part of the universe.

I wonder if David's circumstances caused him to write Psalm 8.

28

Fahgettaboudit!

I woke up this morning humming a tune I would have sworn I had forgotten. It is an old tune from a forgotten album by a music group I'm not sure I remember the name of correctly. It's a catchy song with a great line: "People fail to remember that people tend to forget." In fact, that's the only line I remember from the song.

Psalm 127:2 says that God gives to those he loves, even in their sleep. So what prompted me to wake up with this tune in my mind, only able to remember the words from that one line?

So have I forgotten something? Or what am I failing to remember? Am I counting on someone who has forgotten something, and I need to remember not to be angry? After all, I don't want to fail to remember that people tend to forget?

If you know that I have forgotten something, please forgive me, and, if it is important, remind me. Otherwise, just laugh at my forgetfulness and wonder when I will remember. If you have forgotten something pertaining to me, don't worry about it. I don't remember what it was either.

People fail to remember that people tend to forget—wise words that teach me patience and understanding. Of all the things I fail to remember or tend to forget, I am glad I remember those words.

29

Just Wining

I attended a networking meeting last night. It was a fun time, and I met some wonderful people. I am not a networking type of person but was invited to this one by a new friend, and it sounded like a special group. Each person was asked to bring a bottle of wine. Hors d'oeuvres were served, the wine was opened, and everyone was encouraged to do some tasting.

I am certainly no expert in wine, having been raised in a family that was practically teetotalers. Some of the attendees, however, were experts. They swirled, sniffed, held it up to the light, read the labels ... I tasted several. My mass consumption totaled about half a glass. Sorry to admit, but I would have preferred a diet-soda-tasting event.

When I got home, I decided to do a little—very little—research into wine. I found an article that maintained that the wine in biblical times was probably grape juice. The article went on to prove its point. I was not convinced. It seems like Paul's admonishment to not get drunk with wine loses its point if you render it as "Don't get drunk with grape juice."

Jesus's first miracle also loses some power if you compare serving new to old grape juice.

I have a degree in theology. Sometimes I am ashamed of it when I read theological stuff. It seems to me that Jesus died to bring people into the kingdom of God, and since then, denominations have set up boundaries of belief (and behavior) to try to keep people out.

Jesus's one-word theology was "love." By missing that, I am afraid we have done something nearly as miraculous as Jesus. He turned water into wine, and we have turned wine into grape juice.

30

Stronger than Dirt

I took some time off yesterday morning to do a little yard work. I cut the grass, did some trimming, bundled up some fallen tree limbs, and then put in a little walkway through a flower garden. The walkway meant pulling up some bricks, digging a small trench, and laying some new paver bricks. By the time I was done, I was a sweaty, dirty mess. My hands we covered in caked-on dirt, my shirt and pants were nearly drenched with sweat, and the bill of my cap was constantly dripping.

As I went inside, the only thing on my mind was a shower. Because of the covering of dirt, grass clippings, and sweat that adorned my body, I carefully undressed just inside the back door and headed for the shower. To say it felt good is an understatement. First, it felt good to wash, to get clean, but then it felt good just to stand in the water and feel it run over me. Too bad hot water heaters have limits. I finally got out, dried off, and went about my day.

Maybe I need to take more time and appreciate being clean. I confess, repent, and ask for forgiveness. I do so regularly. Sometimes I know exactly what I have done and feel sorry for; other times it is just the knowledge of being in the world and falling to the conformity I struggle against. But I pray, and he is faithful and just and offers forgiveness. My filth is removed as far as the east is from the west; washed down the drain and gone.

It feels so good to be clean. I must celebrate and give praise for it more often.

31

The Truth Came First

I learned something great this week. It is valuable information that is so simple, and I am sure I already believed it, but it still visited as a revelation.

I am working with a small group of fantastic men who will be doing some mentoring for a local school. It is a great opportunity, and I am looking forward to learning as much as (if not more than) sharing. As we prepared, we discussed the opportunity and the curriculum we will be using. The group is from our church, and we were a little worried about the material because it is faith-based.

One of the members of the group made a fantastic statement that I latched onto. It was something like, "Truth isn't truth just because it is in God's Word, but the truth is the truth, and we know because it is in God's Word." The truth existed first and continues to be the truth, whether it is recorded or not. When God's Word speaks, it is the truth, but the truth came first.

It may not seem like much, but it helps explain that secular realms can have the truth without acknowledging its source. God created the heavens and the earth before it was recorded. It isn't true because it was recorded; rather, it was recorded because it is true. The same is true for love.

I remember reading a book that contained a story of an angel watching a ballerina's perfect performance. She had tremendous talent and was gifted in her performing skill. The angel was confused, knowing that such talent comes from God, but the ballerina gave no glory or thanks to God; rather, she denied his very existence.

The angel was told that the gift and talent came directly from God; that was true. But that fact remained to be true whether the person acknowledged the fact. The fact that the ballerina denied God's existence did not make the truth any less the truth. God was still responsible for her skill.

The truth is inevitable. So is God, denied or not. Praise God for the gift of enduring truth.

32

The Condemned Sin

My latest issue of *Scientific American Mind* came yesterday. I love the magazine, although it always takes an evolution stance, but it has a lot of great material.

This one is a special issue on "The Seven Deadly Sins." I haven't read any of it yet, but I think it is interesting that the magazine is addressing the issue of the sin. I am looking forward to it. By the way, the list is not biblical. It originated with Pope Gregory the Great in the sixth century. . The closest relative to the list of deadly sins biblically is a couple of places in Proverbs, where it talks about things God hates. But it is a large jump from the biblical to the papal.

But even science realizes there is right and wrong behavior. Seems like the scientific world usually just tries to justify "sinful" behavior. In fact, somehow it says some things had been sin but now aren't. Society and culture determine what is right, wrong, ethical, unethical, acceptable, and unacceptable. So where do we draw the lines or redraw the lines? See the problem? Seems it isn't about what God says but the rules we make (and which are open to revision).

Certainly sin is ugly. There is no description of it in which we can say anything good. But I do get concerned with any preoccupation that sin will cause a person to be condemned. Maybe I have stated it before, but condemnation only happens when a person fails to believe in Jesus Christ, which means who he is and what he did.

We know the "Golden Text" of the Bible—John 3:16. "For God so loved the world, that he gave his only Son, that whoever believes in him should not perish but have eternal life." But we can't stop there. "For God did not send his Son into the world to condemn the world, but in order that the world might be saved through him. Whoever believes in him is not condemned, but whoever does not believe is condemned already, because he has not believed in the name of the only Son of God" (John 3:17–18).

Sin doesn't condemn; rather, condemned people sin. Our responsibility is to love; God does. There is a lot more to this, but at least (maybe) this will get you thinking; it has me.

33

My Real Name

Today I do a program at Covenant House for what may be labeled as "at-risk youth." If you're not aware of Covenant House, please look them up; they are a fantastic organization, and the people here in St. Louis are truly amazing.

I am scared to death. I haven't worked with teenagers for a long time, and my nervousness shows. I'm not trying to hide it; I'm not that strong. Not only have I not worked with teenagers for a long time, but these youth are much different from me and have grown up in a much different world than mine.

The people at Covenant House have prepared me and assured me I will do fine. I've planned a program on peer pressure and self-esteem. Although I love the program and believe it's very worthwhile, I'm still nervous. I've worked hard, have activities to reinforce the points, and think it will be a lot of fun and make an impact—but I'm still nervous.

So here is the "thing": I've prayed over this every step of the way. My partner at Covenant House has been praying. I've asked others to pray. My wife reminds me, "I can do all things through him who gives me strength."

Craig Wagganer

So why am I nervous? I've spoken to thousands of people in many different settings. Why should a dozen high-schoolers scare me? God is with me, and I am led by the Holy Spirit in this. What is my problem?

I wonder if, on the day I meet Jesus, he'll call me by name or refer to me as "ye of little faith."

34

Two Priorities

I was reminded of a story. A man was traveling through the jungle when he aroused a sleeping lion. The man began running, but the lion pursued him. The lion steadily gained on the man, who realized there was no way to outrun the lion. The man quickly dropped to his knees and prayed, "Lord, I don't want to die. Please make this lion a Christian lion."

The lion quickly approached but before he pounced, he stopped, looked at the man, and then stared up to heaven and said, "Lord, please make me grateful the food I am about to receive."

I was checking out Facebook correspondence and saw a conversation that disturbed me. It was an argument involving several people, and the debate became heated enough that some questioned the salvation of others. I was disheartened by the way these Christians were treating each other.

Why is it that we, as Christians, sometimes bite and devour one another?

Jesus prayed for two things concerning us when his death was imminent: (1) that the world would know we are his by our love; and (2) that they would be convinced of our message by our unity.

Craig Wagganer

If my words or actions do not promote love and unity, I am not an answer to Jesus's prayer. Somehow, it missed me.

Here is what I believe in my heart of hearts. Jesus died, and God raised him from the dead. Jesus is Lord. If you can agree to that, then despite any other idiosyncrasies either of us has, you're okay with me.

I have a high-powered doctrine gun. And many of my beliefs are unorthodox. But my duty is to love and encourage. I would rather be killed loving than die fighting.

35

This Stuff Works!

What a week! Monday I went to my dad's to get him up and dressed and feed him breakfast. He was in such a weakened state we called the paramedics and took him to the emergency room. He was treated for dehydration and sent home.

On Tuesday, my sister went to care for him and found him as I had, but this time for different reasons. Back to the hospital. This time the situation was more grave. He had a severe urinary tract infection that had become septic, and there was little to do but keep him comfortable. The next day he had progressed and has continued to progress, even though it is very slow. The majority of our time has been spent in the hospital.

We now have to consider rehab facilities and really don't know what the future will hold. We face each situation day by day and try not to speculate on all we don't know and can't foresee.

I was reading in Psalms 119 and came to verse 140: "Your promise is well tried and your servant loves it."

I don't know how people without an abiding faith in the kingdom of God face situations like we have in the past week. I know people believe everything—from "God has never existed" to "God existed but is no longer." Some would say he exists but no longer cares, and some would be more ambivalent and say maybe he exists, but maybe he doesn't.

A deep, abiding faith in the kingdom of God isn't just a simple belief against or without facts. As the psalmist, the biblical authors, and believers ever since have proclaimed, "This works!"

I guess my question isn't "How would people without faith face these situations?"; rather, it's "Why would they?"

36

The Right Location

There are two places I hate to be: hospitals and nursing homes. In the past weeks, I have spent considerable time at both.

My dad went to the hospital with a severe urinary tract infection. His chances were not good, but he responded to medication and progressed. He spent some time in the hospital and then was moved to a rehab unit in a long-term care facility.

Although he is making progress very slowly, he will never return to the condition he was in before the infection. In fact, there is a major concern that when the antibiotics have run their course, the infection will return, which will be fatal.

The two locations I dread were made bearable by Dad's most important location: he is "in Christ." He has received grace (1 Corinthians 1:4); he has been re-created (2 Corinthians 5:17); and he has hope (1 Corinthians 15:22 and 1 Thessalonians 4:16).

Dad and we, his family, have hope. To be in Christ is the one location that supersedes all other locations and guarantees the very best final destination. Every other place is temporary.

37

A Toothless Hiss

The serpent reared his ugly head and struck. The blow was blunt; without any bite. When I turned to look, the head was crushed, and the mouth was open, revealing there were no longer any fangs ...

Dad passed away early this morning. The Enemy came, trying to make a scene, saying that ever since Adam sinned, he has been able claim lives and carry them to the grave. So the grave will be opened, and Satan will try to sneak him in the back door. But Jesus is waiting at the front door, saying, "You can't have him; he's mine."

Death has a terrible hiss but no teeth. The fangs have been removed, so that the mortal blow is just as mortal—it doesn't last. Because of Jesus, the mortal is replaced with immortality. The Enemy's bite has been reduced to a bruise. It hurts, but Jesus heals. It causes death, but Jesus replaces it with life. We do grieve but not as those without hope.

I see Jesus dancing in the graveyard.

38

Caused and Covered

A blanket of snow covers the ground. What was visible yesterday is hidden today. What was there is still there; it is just hidden from our eyes.

We cleaned the front yard the other morning while the weather was nice. We didn't get to the backyard. There are still leaves to rake, dead flowers to pull up, and general cleaning and putting away of things. The snow covers it all. The front, raked and clean, looks exactly like the back, where leaves and plants still are in place.

The grace of God covers all—the best of my ambitions and efforts, as well as the worst inside of me, trying to get out. The grace of God covers it all—my deepest sorrow, which, paradoxically, is my greatest joy. The loss of death is the overwhelming welcome of the certainty of resurrection. The pain of loss, the joy of expectations, grace—maybe it doesn't just cover it all but causes it all.

Dad was sown in tears this week, but Jesus will reap him with shouts of joy!

> When the Lord restored the fortunes of Zion, we were like those who dream. Then our mouth was filled with laughter, and our tongue with shouts of joy; then they said among the nations, "The Lord has done great things for them." The

Lord has done great things for us; we are glad. Restore our fortunes, O Lord, like streams in the Negeb! Those who sow in tears shall reap with shouts of joy! He who goes out weeping, bearing the seed for sowing, shall come home with shouts of joy, bringing his sheaves with him. (Psalm 126:1–6)

39

I Want to Hold Your Hand

My eighteen-month-old granddaughter and I were walking around a local mall. She was holding my hand as we walked down the halls and rode the escalators. We were having a great time; she would often see something, point, and then move in that direction. Once we started on the escalators, it became the fun activity.

As we went up and down and walked along, her attention would often be captured, and she would head in a new direction. I would hold tightly and try to figure out the new interest. Oftentimes it would be in a direction from which I would have to guide her away—such as her propensity of turning around to enter an escalator we had just exited. The sights and smells of Cinnabon was also intriguing to her. She was led to many bright, shiny objects along our stroll.

She held my hand, but if I tried to lead her in a direction away from her interests, she would struggle to get away. I would not let go. There were times when the struggle would get intense enough that I would just pick her up and carry her away.

It made me think. ... Sin happens when inclination meets opportunity.

So I pray, "Lead me not into temptation [opportunity] but deliver me from evil [my inclinations]." I also pray, "Hold my hand so tight I cannot let go; carry me when necessary."

40

Our Simeon Ancestry

Let's stop at the close of the year and reflect on the many possibilities that have come to pass and opportunities we may have missed, and be grateful for every experience we encountered (for each is either a success or a potentially successful learning situation).

I love the story of Simeon in the Bible book of Luke.

Simeon sees the infant Jesus, recognizing the future of the child and his influence upon mankind. After witnessing the presence of the child, Simeon says that he can die in peace, having seen the salvation that God would provide.

What a remarkable realization. Simeon experienced the deepest level of contentment because of the peace he felt in the presence of Jesus and the understanding of salvation.

I wish for you that peace this holiday season. I hope you have a deep, satisfying contentment, and may that peace you experience be the impetus for peace on earth and the display of goodwill toward all.

41

Unwrapping the Gift of Years

It is near the end of the year, and I feel old and very blessed.

Early in December, we celebrated my granddaughter's ninth birthday. We were at a mall, and I took our eighteen-month-old granddaughter for a walk. One of my family took a picture of us as we were walking away. I look old. My shoulders are rounded and I'm starting to slump forward.

This past year, my body has started to turn against me; the aches and pains have gotten worse, and I had to have neck surgery. Above the neck I find myself at a loss—losing my hair, my teeth, my hearing, and my eyesight. I haven't lost my mind, but I do tend to misplace it more often than I used to.

On the other hand, I look at my wonderful wife. She continues to grow more beautiful—in form, character, and spirit—with every passing day, so the years are remarkable!

We celebrated our 40th anniversary in 2015. She has given me the gift of her youthful passion and exuberance. She has shared her stability, compassion, and grace. She offers a tremendous wisdom and perspective I can't live without.

Craig Wagganer

I have many blessings to count as the end of the year comes, but I'm most grateful for one thing in two ways—the gift of years. One, I came to know Jesus as a teenager. I treasure the years I have had with him. Two, I came to love Shirley as a teenager. I treasure the years I have had with her.

I'm getting older; Jesus and Shirley are getting better. I treasure the memories and look forward to more years.

42

Years Ago, This Was the Future

We are an instant society. We want everything as soon as possible, if not sooner. Even though it is killing us slowly, we want to be able to go through the drive-through to get our fast food faster. I know I have sometimes grown impatient with the microwave for taking so long. We all have our own illustrations.

But what about something that takes a while to develop before we see the results?

Today is Shirley's birthday. We'll celebrate with the family this evening. Who would have known when she was born the changes that she would make in the world.

When Shirley was born no one knew what the future would hold for her. Anyone who knows me knows I am better off—and just plain better—because she came into the world. Because she changed me, she changed my world, my perspective of it, and thereby everyone around it.

Everyone who knows her is better off by her acquaintance. And the world around us changes; it is better. John Donne said correctly, "No man is an island ..." We are all part of the whole;

Craig Wagganer

we're connected, and people like Shirley make connections worthwhile.

I love Shirley. When I celebrate her birthday, I am celebrating one of the greatest days of my life.

One day can change the future in the future; it just takes time.

43

A Positive Calendar

It was a pleasure to speak at the Christian Church of Olney, Illinois, last Sunday. They have a great group, and it was fun to visit and have the opportunity to be with them. As I prepared for my Sunday with them, I let my thoughts take me where they led, and I wound up with a message on how to change attitude. I used a cartoon—which I am sure Shirley would say was a true story—that I saw at my last doctor visit. It showed a patient sitting on the exam table and the doctor looking at his report. The doctor says to the man, "You tested positive for being negative."

So I came upon a strategy I promised to use in my own life and challenged others as well. Here is what I am going to do:

Monday—spend some time thinking of three things I am thankful for. This isn't a quick thanks and on with my life. This is seriously thinking of three things I am truly grateful for and diving deep into the reasons why. This is to be a serious dissection, not a flippant activity.

Tuesday—a day to reflect on a positive experience. This can be something recent or something more historical; either way, it is designed to help me value past experiences and their meanings to me.

Wednesday—this is a day to think and dream about the future in a positive way. It may be about an upcoming activity or something I would like to plan. It may be about the promises of God; it may be about an afternoon with the grandkids. It just needs to be positive thoughts about the future.

Thursday—note-writing day. On this day, I write someone important in my life a brief note. It may be thanks or encouragement or maybe even "Get well" or "Looking forward to seeing you." But I will take time to write a note and mail it.

Friday—a day of reflection on what I've experienced. I'll record either a positive experience or take a negative experience and write out the positive lessons I learned.

I purchased a 2014 daily calendar to record each day's activities. Four days in, and I am doing well. But I have found that doing the days as I've outlined them has led me to anticipate the next day and days. It seems I go through each day a little every day. I've found it to be a good thing.

Here is how I've outlined my week; it's easy to keep track:

Monday—Thanksgiving
Tuesday—Terrific Times
Wednesday—Fantastic Future
Thursday—Dear ...
Friday—Review or Reframe

I look forward to these activities either improving my outlook or at least teaching me some valuable lessons. I'll let you know how it goes.

44

Little Lamps, Shining Lights

How dangerous it must be to know the future. What if I knew everything that was going to happen to me, for example, for the next ten years? The reason I say it would be dangerous is because of recent thinking. What if ten years ago I had known all that would come to pass in my life over these past ten years? Moving from Minnesota to Atlanta to St. Louis … the birth of three grandchildren … the death of both my parents and one of Shirley's … the disappointments and dreams of different jobs and responsibilities … the gains and the losses. To think about all the details is overwhelming. If I had known in advance, it would have been debilitating—too much information.

Psalm 119 says that God's words lead us like a lamp illuminating our feet; a light that reveals the path. At the time of the writing they didn't have the flashlights we have now that can almost light up the moon. The light the psalmist is talking about only shed light a short distance.

I know God has informed us about the future kingdom of God as our ultimate hope, but other than that, I think God guides us step by step. Faith is moving forward, trusting every step into the Master's hand. It isn't a grand knowledge that provides insight into future events, other than to trust him every step as we get there.

Craig Wagganer

My danger is looking too far forward to where the light hasn't shined yet, and the darkness scares me. I need to look where the light shines, be confident, and move forward. My feet must be in the path where the light is shining; my hand must be holding the one who guides and my heart trusting the one who loves and knows and has seen the next ten years. He'll reveal what I need to know, see, and do.

"The heart of man plans his way, but the Lord establishes his steps" (Proverbs 16:9).

45

Influencing Bithia

Everyone knows Moses and the powerful leadership he exemplified. Even people with little acquaintance with the Bible know his story. But have you ever thought about the power of influence that was evident around him?

We know that Moses's mom, Jochebed, put him in a basket and set him in the Nile River. We also know that his sister, Miriam, stood watch, waiting to see what would happen. Pharaoh's daughter came along, and we know the rest of the story ... or do we?

While we know and wonder at the leadership shown by Moses, we may have overlooked just how powerfully influential some others in the story might have been.

Moses was the right person for the job of leading the Israelites out of Egypt. Having been raised in the pharaoh's household, he would have been accustomed to that culture. But in being raised by his mother, he was also educated in the ways of the people of Israel and their history. He spent forty years wandering in the wilderness of Sinai, herding sheep, so he was well-suited to make the trek, leading his people. When you look at his life, you can see God preparing him for his unique calling and task.

But how important Jochebed and Miriam are. First Chronicles 4:17 is a little verse that informs us that one of the people "exodusing" from Egypt was none other than Pharaoh's daughter Bithia. She married an Israelite and had a child named (get this) Miriam! Of course, it is only speculation, but the influence of the godly woman Jochebed and her daughter, Miriam, was so strong that even Pharaoh's daughter understood their light, chose to leave her position, married a Hebrew slave, and named a child according to her influencers.

By the way, Bithia is not listed among the lineage of Christ. But she married into the tribe of Judah, so she is probably a great-aunt or something.

Jochebed is barely mentioned in the Moses story and biblical record. But there is little doubt that her influence will be celebrated in the coming kingdom.

Please be aware how powerful your influence can be. Let your light so shine before men.

46

Pass? Stay?

I came across a phrase while reading in the Bible book of Joshua. The phrase was, "It came to pass." It stuck out in my mind because it seemed very familiar but also new. I guess the reason is that in the King James Bible, which I grew up with, it was a recurring phrase, but in the English Standard Version, it only appears twice (as far as I can tell).

I got to thinking about that phrase. It seems like that is good way to look at things. Certain situations arise, circumstances can be difficult, problems arise, but it will come to pass. In fact, if we look back over our lives, we see that all our problems came to pass. Think about that wording for a moment; there's a couple different meanings altogether true.

In reality, all things come to pass—good or bad, they pass. We know that every problem, every sorrow, and every negative thing will come to pass. But we also realize that almost every good thing also will come to pass.

The apostle Paul writes that three thing remain: faith, hope, and love. But faith will come to pass. When Jesus returns, we will see him face-to-face. We will know as we are known, and our knowledge will be made complete; our faith replaced by sight. Faith will come to pass.

Craig Wagganer

Hope will come to pass. When Jesus returns, that which we hope for and long for with groanings too deep for words—that hope will pass away. Where we once hoped and longed for the kingdom of God, we will have the experience and reality of being there.

As I thought about it, there were only a few things that didn't or don't come to pass. Love is here to stay. The most powerful force in the world will only increase with the return of Christ.

I wonder about you and me and others—are we coming to pass or coming to stay?

The kingdom of God will not come to pass; it will come to stay.

47

Good Advice from the Doc

A cousin was passing through town the other day, and I met him and his wife for supper. During the evening's conversation, a story came up of how I once ate some spoiled shrimp and got very sick.

The shrimp-noodle dish was about a week old. I took it out of the refrigerator, didn't bother to warm it up, and began to eat. As I was eating, I thought that it tasted a little fuzzy, but that didn't give me reason to pause. I kept eating. An hour or so later, I was praying the biblical prayer from the book of Jonah: "It is better for me to die than to live." And, with groanings, I thought I was beyond healing and was ready to pass.

I saw a review of the movie *The Wolf of Wall Street*. At first, it sounded like the kind of movie I might enjoy. But then the review said that this movie set a record for profanity and soft-core nudity.

If putting something spoiled into my digestive system can make me so sick that I would pray for death as a relief, how much more might my mind be made sick by putting into it something profane? I truly don't understand why filmmakers continue to push this envelope, and I don't understand people's desire to see such films. Are we not familiar with the "garbage in/garbage out" principle? Do we not understand that what we see, what we might call entertainment, comes into us and affects us?

Craig Wagganer

Doc Campbell of *Hee Haw* fame was once confronted by a patient who desperately announced, "Doctor, Doctor, I broke my arm in two places." The good doc's reply was simple: "Well, stay out of them places!"

First Corinthians 15:33 warns that bad company corrupts good morals. And Psalms 101:3 gives good advice: "I will not set before my eyes anything that is worthless."

48

A Little Boy, a Boat, and a Father

The rain came down pretty hard yesterday but only for a short time. I was watching out a window as the sides of the streets looked like little streams with a fast-moving current. As I watched, I was reminded of a favorite story.

During a prolonged rainy afternoon, a small boy found his way to his father's tools in the basement. Taking a few pieces of wood and some other materials, he fashioned a beautiful little boat, complete with a dowel-rod mast and a handkerchief sail. He found some paint and markers and completed his project.

A little while later, as it was getting dark, the rain stopped. The little boy hurried outside and began to play with his boat as the water ran down the street. In the darkness and the speed of the moving water, the little boat got away from the sailor and was washed down a storm sewer. The little guy was crushed.

A week or so had passed when the boy and his mom were walking down the street, and the boy saw his ship sitting in a resale shop window. With urgent pleas, the boy took his own money and bought back the boat. He felt love and pride as he walked out of the store.

He held up his creation and exclaimed, "Little boat, little boat, you are mine twice. I made you, and I bought you."

Craig Wagganer

First John 3 begins by asking us to see and understand the kind of love our heavenly Father has given to us, for we are called the children of God. We are his twice—he made us, and he has bought us.

49

Coffee-Cup Guidance

I got up, made breakfast, and, as Shirley left for work, I decided to run by the library to return some movies before they opened to avoid being charged a fine. I had some change in my pocket and drove through McDonald's and treated myself to a cup of their fresh-brewed decaf.

Once home, I sat at my desk and opened my Bible to the day's readings, starting in Numbers 1. I came across the phrase, concerning a census, "able to go to war." I wondered ... would I be listed as someone able to go to war for the people of God? I might come back to that thought later. About then, something else happened.

As I leaned forward with my Bible in front of me, pondering those words and those thoughts, I took a drink of coffee and sat the cup on my desk at the edge of the Bible. When I looked at the printing on the cup, I saw an arrow, preceded by the words, "Good days start here." The arrow seemed to be pointing at my Bible.

Good days start here. I get it.

50

The Order of Things

This past week I attended the funeral of a friend. It was great to hear many stories about this woman and her legacy. It was also nice to see family and friends gathered from so many places to show their love and support. The church was packed to standing room only.

Also, this past week was busy as we finally cleaned out my dad's house. He passed away last November, and it's been a slow process going through his and my mom's belongings and getting the house empty so that repairs can be made before putting it on the market. This week it was hauling things to their new locations.

I also had a birthday. In reality, I was only a day older, but it is celebrated as a year. It seemed like more.

The death of a friend, the closing and final removal of a lifetime of accumulation, the passing of another year.

The Bible says that a life is like a vapor, a mist, a blade of grass.

I was reading in the book of Numbers how the people of Israel were to break camp, move, and then set up camp. There are lots of interesting details, but one thing I noticed—as they were to set out, there was a definite order. And one reason for the order was so that as they came to make camp, the tabernacle would arrive in time to set up the tent before the temple furnishings arrived. When the *holy things* arrived, the tent was ready for them to be put in place.

Jesus went ahead of us, he said, to prepare a place for us. What great order has God's plan. What tremendous blessing in searching it out, in seeking it first.

51

Run!

For some time I have believed that sin happens when opportunity meets inclination. Opportunity is the time when we are placed in a situation where temptation calls us and seeks to seduce us. We all have inclinations to sin; that is, temptations that haunt us, follow us, and present themselves to us.

If I have the opportunity for sin but don't have inclinations toward that opportunity, then I can resist. If I have the inclination toward a sin (and we all do), the best I can do is avoid any opportunity for my inclinations to take over. Sin happens when opportunity meets inclination; remove one or the other, and we can have victory.

In praying the Lord's Prayer, we say, "Don't lead us into temptation, but deliver us from evil." Jesus taught us to pray that we would not come to situations where we would be tempted; keep us away from opportunities to sin. And he taught us to pray that we would be delivered from our bent toward sinning—our inclinations.

Joseph, in the Bible book of Genesis, is faced by a temptation from one of the most powerful women in Egypt. His choice was to run. A very wise example from the Old Testament concerning when opportunity meets inclination ... *run!*

52

Core Grace

I found a chair that looked out the airport window and sat down to relax while waiting for my aircraft to arrive. As usual, I was early and had time to do some reading.

As I sat down, I noticed a *USA Today* newspaper a few seats from me. Holding it up, with the bottom of the newspaper in my lap, I moved through the pages, skimming the articles' headlines. I was almost to the last section when an apple core fell out of the pages, hit my leg, and fell to the floor.

At first, I was a little angered. What kind of person would put an apple core between the pages of a newspaper and leave it on a chair for someone else to find? After just a second of thought, I had a resulting thought: maybe this was a prank, and someone (or two) was watching to see what would happen. I then realized I had choices to make. How would I respond to the situation?

You can come up with as many scenarios as you wish. I probably thought of the same ones as you are now. Here's what I did: I reached down, picked up the core, and placed it on the windowsill in front of me. It would be out of the way there, and no one else would have to deal with it. I folded the paper, after removing the "juiced" pages. I then pulled out a book and began to read. I did not look around. I did not make any gestures or react in any other way.

Some movement caught my attention; it was my plane arriving at the gate. I waited for the flight to be called and then packed up my belongings and picked up the apple core and the stained paper. As I moved toward the gate, I placed the waste in the trash bin. Then, on to the plane, finally headed home.

On the plane, I wondered again about the apple. Who placed the apple there for me to find? Did anyone? Perhaps it was God. Maybe he placed it there to see how I would handle the situation. That paper may not have existed for anyone else who sat there. Or maybe the paper was there but without an apple inside. Was this a situation just for me?

Hebrews 13:2 says, "Do not neglect to show hospitality to strangers, for thereby some have entertained angels unawares." Could an application be, "Do not neglect to show hospitality in nonhospitable situations"? Is this what grace is all about?

53

Future Realities Impact Present Ideologies

Many years ago, in college, there was a great debate on what makes a person who he or she is. Is it genetics or environment? One school of thought said a person becomes what he or she is because of genetics. A person is the sum of the gene pool that he or she comes from. The other school believed that a person is the result of the environment in which he or she lived. Was it nature or nurture?

In the discussions, most people would finally say that it was a combination; then the argument would turn to percentages. How much of each was involved, and which was of more importance?

I think there is a third factor—the future. A person is who he is—or more correctly, what he becomes—partly because of genetics, partly because of the environment, and largely because of what he believe about the future. A person that believes in a bright future approaches life differently from a person who has a bleak outlook.

A growing part of me is determined about how I see the future. I believe that Jesus will return to the earth and establish God's kingdom. I believe that's the promise to all who believe in their hearts and confess with their mouths.

That belief has a determining factor in who I am now and what I am becoming.

In the Bible book of Matthew 5, Jesus says that certain people are blessed now for what they will receive in the future. It isn't that they will be blessed, but they are blessed. They aren't in blessed situations, but they are blessed in anticipation of what they will receive. That is the power of hope. That is the power of the future that changes things now.

Being salt and light in the world means that I recognize my present blessed position in anticipation of future realities. There is no denying my genetic makeup. I am also sure that the environment in which I grew up impacted me. But a powerful force influencing me now is my belief and hope concerning the future.

Maybe that is what seeking the kingdom of God first is all about.

54

God's Mark

I've had the pleasure of babysitting grandchildren twice this week. And it is a pleasure to spend time with them and watch them and enjoy their presence. It is enlightening to talk with them, see what makes them tick, what they're interested in, and what they think is fair and unfair.

Each one is so very different. They're in the same house, same parents and surrounding, but each is different and has special qualities unique to that child. Last night I had some alone time with each one. It was an education for me just to learn and experience each child's individuality. I won't go into my observations, but Hannah (nine years old), Ben (six years), and Sarah (two at the end of the month) have taught me a lot and continue to shape me.

Last night, after kissing them good night, praying with them, and turning out the lights, I had some alone time. I had to be beaming as I thought about the evening and how much I love those little folks. I thought about their differences and how special each one is.

It dawned on me how special each person is. Created in the image of God and shaped by forces we don't and can't understand, we are totally unique. Because of past experiences, I judge people quickly. I make assumptions, draw conclusions, and then treat people not how they deserve but according to my (very limited and finite) understanding of what I think and prejudge about them. How unfair I am.

I need to value each individual. I need to understand them, their idiosyncrasies, and their reflections of the image of God.

The world would be a better place if I would treat everyone like I treat my grandchildren. I think it is worth a try.

55

The Gift of Empty

What are your favorite gifts you've ever received?

Thoughts probably go back to a magical Christmas morning, or a favorite birthday, or maybe a time when you received something unexpected for no reason at all. Maybe you remember the gift because of the special occasion on which it was given, or maybe the thoughtfulness involved, or because it was given by a very special person.

What makes a gift special? Is it the actual gift, the occasion, the giver, or something I haven't even mentioned? Maybe it was the situation you were in—the circumstances surrounding the gift. What is it that makes a gift special or memorable or the greatest gift ever?

Can you imagine receiving a gift you weren't expecting? Then full of anticipation, you open it and ... *surprise!* The gift box is empty! Would you consider that the greatest gift ever?

The greatest gift I ever received was an empty tomb.

Jesus, come back soon. I'm looking forward to more empty tombs.

56

Still Rolls the Stone

Last Sunday's Easter celebration was really special at the church I attend. The music and message was a real reinforcement of the truth of the Bible about the resurrection of Jesus and the hope of salvation. And it was also a phenomenal time to be with my brothers and sisters in the faith, sharing a great experience.

We sang a song you might be familiar with, the words of which contain the phrase, "My God is awesome; he can move mountains."

Those words stuck with me throughout the service and into the afternoon, even to today.

Don't get me wrong; I believe them and trust them. I know God can move mountains and even more so that he is awesome. But his awesomeness, for me, isn't because he can move mountains; it's because he rolled away a stone.

57

Details, Details, Details

This week has been hectic. I have two programs in five days, and there's quite a bit to get ready. My problem is that I'm not really a details kind of person, so I am always sweating that I have missed or overlooked something. I keep checking my list, but I'm still not at ease until I get the program started.

To say I'm not a details kind of person is certainly not to be critical of those who are detail-oriented. In fact, I could have saved a lot of problems and my current state of nervousness if I were more into the details. I've worked hard to make the progress I have, and I think I have come a long way. But, admittedly, there is still room. I'll keep working on it. I have become more of a list maker, and I check things twice.

Reading the book of Leviticus, it is clear that God is in the details. His instructions are clear and concise regarding the laws he would have govern the post-Egypt Israelites. They are demanding, and it is clear he wanted no misunderstanding in their execution. The details make it clear that God is there.

Craig Wagganer

As I get ready for tomorrow and next week, I have to make sure all the details are cared for. I can't afford to overlook something that might be a critical component to the success of the event.

God never overlooks the details. He knows the end from the beginning; even the hairs on my head. Every detail, God has taken care of. I guess I can rest, knowing that.

58

Challenging Cartoons

Preparing to speak at a church conference this week has been overwhelming. When I used to prepare messages weekly, I had a routine, and it became pretty easy. But now, only speaking on special occasions seems to be hard work. Praying and trying to decide on messages is difficult because there is so much material and so little time.

I was asked to speak on a spring theme, like renewal. My preparations have taken me from several Old Testament passages to several New Testament passages. I get started on one thing, and then a new train of thought comes up. Then I think, *I should just speak on what I am going through personally; how God is directing me.*

What to do?

Since the beginning of the year, I have been trying to improve my attitude. Two cartoons caught my attention. One was a *Calvin and Hobbes,* where Calvin resolves that life needs more dance numbers and special effects. The other is a person whose doctor has just informed him that he tested positive for being negative.

I am afraid the results of my test may find the same thing, so I resolved to have more dance numbers and special effects in my life. The last few months have been a search to figure out how to do just that.

So this week I'll speak twice, and we'll focus on experiencing more celebrations and miracles. We'll dive into the book of Philippians and have some very practical prescriptions for a negative attitude.

In the meantime, give these words of Winston Churchill a think: "The positive thinker sees the invisible, feels the intangible, and achieves the impossible." Sounds a bit like Philippians 4:13.

59

What's in a Name?

Last week, Shirley and I traveled across the state to speak at a church conference. It was a wonderful weekend, with a gracious church as host and a wonderful family who put us up for the weekend.

As we traveled across the state, I began noticing all the churches along the way. And then I started paying attention to the names. So many, many churches and so many names.

Many seemed to have the traditional type of names, such as First Church of Columbia. Others were traditional congregations with traditional names—First Methodist Church of Boonville.

Others had a moniker attached to them, such as Peter, Paul, Stephen, Joseph, Mary, Phillip, Mary Magdalene, and, of course, God and Jesus.

We saw Country Side, Country Way, Country View and, accordingly, City, City Wide, City View—even a City Lights. Some had "Bible" in their names, like Bible Way, Bible Truth, Bible Assembly, and—not to be outdone—Open Bible.

Then there were the more creative names—Epic, Journey, Cowboy, Way, Kingdom, Victory, Harvest, Enjoy, Injoy, Celebration. I wish we would have written them down.

Craig Wagganer

There were also "virtue" churches. These carried names like Peace, Mercy, Grace, and Faith.

My first thought was, *With so many churches across the state, why do I see so little difference?*

I reverted back to thinking about church names. I thought, *When I get home, I'm going to do some research into church names and see how many I can find.* I haven't done it yet.

There was one very important word I didn't see in any church name, however, and I couldn't remember seeing it in a church name ever in my life. The word obviously missing—have you thought of it?—is *love*.

I don't believe I have ever seen a "Love Church." I wondered why. I suppose the pressure would be too great.

60

The Toothpaste Test

I was with a young man who'd had a particularly bad morning. It was definitely noticeable, and he was carrying a chip on his shoulder, wanting to punish everyone around him for the circumstances causing his personal pain.

I thought of a story told by the late Howard Hendricks at a Promise Keepers event. A man approached Dr. Hendricks, who asked, "How's it going?" The man replied, "Pretty good, under the circumstances." Dr. Hendricks's quick-witted reply was, "Well, what are you doing under there?"

It is so easy to get "under the circumstances." Situations happen that may be out of our control and may place us in positions we don't like and would prefer not to be in. We have to take action, but the usual action is to complain and wait. We don't like being "under the circumstances," but it is easier to feel sorry for ourselves and solicit pity than it is to quickly address the situation, take responsibility, and take positive action.

Joseph of the biblical book of Genesis was a man who faced adversity—some of his own doing and some as a result of doing the right thing. He was sold into slavery for his youthful arrogance and evoking the jealousy of ten of his brothers. Then, rising to power in Egypt, he abruptly ran from the presence of temptation, and, because of false testimony, was thrown in jail. There's a lot more to the story of Joseph—you can check it out in Genesis 37–50.

But the verses in Psalm 105:16–22 that tell a little more of Joe's story. There's a little phrase in verse 19: "the Lord tested him."

Could it be a test? What I'm going through now, the circumstances I'm under—could they be a test? Is God squeezing me like toothpaste to see what's inside? Have I cast all my cares upon him that he may care for me? Am I trusting in the Lord with all my heart? Have I abandoned my own perspectives to acknowledge and recognize him in every circumstance, that he may direct me?

I am not to be under anything but on top, to the praise and glory of the Lord. I know he can handle it—and me.

61

Getting a Head Start(ed)

I found myself thinking about thinking. How does it work? What are thoughts? How do we think? How does memory work? How do we remember things? Even more confusing, why can't I remember what I know when I want to? Why does it escape my grasp?

How do I train my mind to think only the things I want it to? How can I keep it from wandering; from being distracted by little things? How can I focus? Why can some focus better than others? Why does it seem like I am seldom able to concentrate and too often chase my mind, trying to keep it under control?

All these questions because I'd read Philippians 4:8, "Whatever is honorable, whatever is just, whatever is pure, whatever is lovely, whatever is commendable, if there is any excellence, if there is anything worthy of praise, think about these things."

How do I do that?

Maybe if I take a look at each word and try to find an example or illustration, that might help me to understand the concept or the principle, and then I could focus, understand, and apply.

So what is honorable? The dictionary uses noble as a synonym. So that would render Isaiah 32:8 as, "But he who is honorable plans honorable things, and on honorable things he stands." So my mind needs to think about honorable things. To plan how to do them. To take notice and evaluate activities to see if they are honorable and, if not, change my course.

The book of Proverbs seems to equate honor with honesty and integrity. To be honorable is to be of good character, high integrity, and good morality. I need to think about these things. To plan, act, and judge accordingly.

Thinking is dangerous. Choosing to be careful about what you think is strenuous. But it is noble if you are filling your thoughts and activities with honorable things.

62

Just Thinking

I read where habits are formed in the mind. Repeatedly doing something is akin to making channels in your brain. The more you do something, the deeper the channel; the more established the habit. That automatic behavior that is the habit is something you do almost without thinking; it becomes so routine that it just happens. If the habit includes action, there is even something called muscle memory—not that your actual muscles have memory capabilities, but the continued or repeated activity develops your muscle groups for that activity.

Philippians 4:8 says we are to think about what is "just." Interesting word—it can mean several things, but two meanings reappear with regularity in the Bible. One has to do with what is morally right, and the other meaning conveys the word "exactly."

Several times, the word is used when someone did just (exactly) as the Lord commanded. The important thing to note is that you can't do exactly according to something without knowing exactly what the directions are. So to do exactly as the Lord commanded means you have to be familiar with what the Lord commands.

Some biblical characters are described as being just, meaning they acted in a morally right and proper fashion. Used as an adjective, "just" describes the habitual behavior that comes from a person's character. Over time, character develops habits, and habits are displayed in behavior.

Both of these uses mean we must familiarize ourselves with what God desires. Otherwise, thinking and doing what is "just" and doing it "just" as the Lord asks is open to our own interpretations, thoughts, and feelings.

Micah 6:8 says, "He has told you, O man, what is good; and what does the Lord require of you but to do justice, and to love kindness, and to walk humbly with your God."

To be just—to do justice—a person must think about what is just, and that thinking will guide activities. Those activities will then become descriptors of the person's character. Philippians requests that we think about what is just; it is the first step in developing habits in the mind that will lead to just behavior.

63

Memorial Stones

Shirley and I were looking at some flowers blooming in our little garden. The irises and a couple things I don't know the names of were quite lovely. As we looked I saw a little craft project we'd done with the grandkids last summer.

We'd taken some concrete, mixed it up, and put it in a little square mold. Then we added different color stones to it, let it set up, and *voilà!*

Each of the kids made one to take home, and they made one for Shirley and I to bring home. We set it in our little flower patch, and each time we enjoy the beauty, we also are reminded of a great time with our fantastic grandchildren.

It reminded me of the importance of history, remembering, and memorials. When we were in Israel, we noticed while driving through the desert that we would see a few larger stones piled up on each other—a stack of three, four, or five. At the cemeteries, there would be graves with the same type of stone pile or a single stone placed on top of the marker.

When we asked our guide about these strange configurations, he told us that each was placed there as a memorial and marker to say that something significant happened there. It gave us a new appreciation for these little testimonies as we recognized them on the rest of the trip. The little craft project that adorns our garden gives us a little pause each time we see it, reminding us of a special moment back in 2013. It is a wonderful thing.

In the Bible book of Joshua 4, the Israelites are told to place memorial stones regarding their crossing of the Jordan into the Promised Land; Joshua 4:6 tells the reason why.

We need to incorporate this type of thing into our lives. We may forget to pass on lessons we learn, but if we place reminders to let people know, then they can ask, we'll remember, and the story can be told—the lesson passed.

What's your story if people ask, "Why?"

64

Psycho Pure

Our refrigerator has a water purifier built into it. It's amazing how much cleaner the water that goes through the purifier is. A long time ago, we bought a purifier that was attached to a two-quart pitcher. The first time we used it, we were speechless. The water seemed to be clearer, even brighter than the tap water. At that point, we lived on a farm, and the water was from a well; there was a big different. Now we are on city water, but the difference when using the purifier is still noticeable.

Now, I am not saying this because I'm on a clean-water rave, but Philippians 4:8 says to think on things that are pure. When I think of pure, I think of crystal-clear water. So when I am advised to think about pure things, I think of things that are free from any pollutants; things that have no contaminants. Just as pure water refreshes and is good for the body, pure thoughts refresh and are good for the spirit. Just like pure water that you can see through clearly, pure thoughts are undefiled.

This is pretty hard in our culture. We are bombarded by impurities. They are unavoidable. We do well to recognize them and even better to run from them, not giving them a chance to take a foothold within our thoughts. So hard ... no wonder the Philippians author is so concerned.

Craig Wagganer

Eliphaz asks a great question in Job 4:17. "Can a man be pure before his maker?" Psalm 119:9 seems to help us in our quest: "How can a young man keep his way pure? By guarding it according to your word."

I need to constantly keep up my guard against impurities. And God's Word is the filter I must know and use to make sure my mind is stayed on pure things.

65

Flowery Thoughts

Shirley and I took a trip to the botanical gardens in St. Louis. It was a beautiful day, and we really enjoyed the flowers and the butterflies; they even have a great Lego exhibit.

Yesterday I was downloading some pictures from a recent trip and noticed the pictures I had taken at the garden. I'm not much of a photographer, but the flowers were absolutely beautiful. As I scanned through the pictures, I enjoyed looking them and remembering the trip. One word I kept hearing myself say was, "Lovely."

The flowers were lovely—attractive or beautiful, especially in a graceful way (according to a dictionary definition). And they were attractive and beautiful, and there was a definite grace about their beauty and splendor of colors and surroundings.

To think about such lovely things is an exercise in training the mind to recognize what is favorable and pleasing, as well as its being an opportunity to experience God's grace in a little different way. Philippians 4:8 says to think about what is lovely. It can be the practice of the presence of God.

66

Thinking Habits

A lot of things have been recommended to me. I think it is natural, when you have a good experience, to recommend that pleasurable experience to others. It is normal to recommend restaurants, foods, books, places, people, events ... the list could go on. Every good experience can become a recommendation to others.

Philippians 4:8 says we are to think about things that are commendable. I don't think the author is saying we should think about things that have been recommended to us by our friends and associates. But what is commendable? What is recommended for us to gather our thoughts around? What did the author of Philippians mean when he advised us?

Commendable things on which I should focus ... hmmm ... serious thinking ... So I must decide commendable versus noncommendable; virtue versus valueless. It's much more than restaurants, books and movies. It is the thinking that determines my destiny.

Would I commend to others what I am thinking about? Some changes might need to be made.

67

Screening Thoughts

Yesterday my brother-in-law and I shopped for and bought my mother-in-law a new TV. Why are there so many choices? We only went to one store, but the choices were overwhelming. She wanted a flat screen—well, that's all they make now. She had a 28-inch screen, and she wanted something a little larger. A 40-inch was fine, but what about a 32-inch model?

After looking, we decided the 40-inch would be best and still fit nicely on her small entertainment center. After looking at several, we came across some 39-inch versions. Really? A 39-inch and a 40-inch screen from the same manufacturer? At first, it was laughable how many choices there were at just this one store—and then, how many stores sell TVs?

After installing the TV and getting it all set up, I drove home. Along the way, I became very sad. Going into a consumer-electronics store just to buy a TV can be overwhelming. I didn't grow up with this stuff but still become ensnared in the trappings. How will future generations be—those that grow up with a sense of entitlement to all the gadgets and enslaved to have the biggest, the best, the latest?

Today is the Fourth of July. We'll enjoy outdoor games, cookouts, swimming pools, water guns, and family and friends, and we'll cap it off with fireworks. TVs will be abandoned, replaced by fun activities and visiting. Maybe we should celebrate more days every day.

Philippians 4:8 says we should think about excellent things. I just don't think TV makes the cut.

68

Always Blooming

Can you imagine being married to the same person for thirty-nine years? No way—how boring, how mundane.

Thirty-nine years ago tomorrow (July 12), Shirley and I got married. Little did I know or understand when I said "I do" that it would always be in the present tense. "I do" every day, because what I didn't understand then, I do now. I wasn't going to be married to the same woman forever; she would change and grow and become more than I even dreamed at that point in time.

I'm not married to the same person; that girl has become a woman. That shy girl has become a woman and model of virtue. I didn't realize then, but I do as I look back, that I was marrying great possibilities and potential. She has grown, matured, and led me to be better than I would have ever been without her. I didn't know that she was making an investment in me, and now she has paid dividends beyond my expectations.

I'll hear someone say that they've been married to the same person for "x" mount of years. That's a shame. I've been married to a growing woman, whose been growing me for thirty-nine years. She's not the same as she was thirty-nine years ago; she's better. Thankfully, I'm

Craig Wagganer

not the same as I was thirty-nine years ago either. Her influence has helped me grow too.

Last year I bought Shirley a beautiful purple coneflower. In a year, it has tripled in size. The flowers are fantastic. God designed things to be nourished and to grow. Certainly, God designed Shirley.

69

Changed Stones

I stopped by the cemetery the other day. I wanted to see if my dad's dates had been engraved on his marker. As I looked at the stone, I began to wonder what would happen to all the stones in that cemetery—all the cemeteries. One day there will be no graves, no grave markers.

My first thought was that I would like the steps of my abode in God's kingdom to be headstones. You see, that's what headstones really are. They mark a step in the process. To conquer death, you only have to die. It's just a step in the process. In a very real way, they aren't headstones; they're stepping stones. They mark a person who has taken the next step.

Now, I know the verses in the Bible that talk about the new heavens and new earth; the ones that say this earth and everything in it will melt away in fervent heat. But in that kingdom of limitless possibilities, I would like to think that I'll be able to take a walk through that cemetery and others, where loved ones are napping, and look at the holes left by the resurrection. Maybe the information on the headstones will be changed to read something like this (in the case of my dad): "Amos Wagganer slept here."

70

Live Bread

I met a friend at a local Bread Company. We visited for an hour or so, and as I was leaving, I purchased a loaf of honey-wheat bread. I had it sliced in their wide slice machine and took it home. So far, I've used it for French toast as well as regular toast and for a sandwich. It is really good; I have really enjoyed it.

In the Bible book of John 6, Jesus refers to himself as the bread of life. He does so at least five times, depending on the version you choose. I could certainly run analogies too far and into the ground. But one of the things I like about bread (and I love bread) is that it is versatile.

French toast, regular toast, sandwiches, with gravy, with butter, to push the last tiny bite of food left on the plate onto the fork ... I was surprised at one point in my life that some people didn't know that if you butter a piece of bread and then wrap it around a freshly steamed ear of corn and rotate it a little, you not only have a melted-butter bread but a perfectly buttered ear of corn.

Bread is great. Jesus is the bread of life. Whatever my need or situation, Jesus is versatile; he can handle me. I am grateful for bread; I'm eternally thankful for the bread of life.

71

Small Hurt, Major Pain

It's just a small bone, maybe not even a bone but bone growth from a long-past injury, a kind of scar tissue type of thing. Whatever it is, it's broken. I had what I thought was a bruise on the side of my foot for about a day, and then one step and *pop*. Now I can't put any weight on it, and the doc says eight to twelve weeks for healing.

As I said, a very small bone or bone chip on the outside and underside of my right foot. Considering the size of the rest of my body, how can something so small hurt so bad?

I need to pay more attention to people at church who are hurting. And not the obvious hurts that are mentioned but the pain in peripheral people who are hurting. Considering the size our church is becoming, I need to make sure I'm paying attention. I need to make sure to take care of every need before it becomes a major pain (1 Corinthians 12:26–27).

72

Nicknamed by Jesus

Twice this week I have heard someone mention Jesus's family. Both times they mentioned the pressure that his younger siblings must have felt. Imagine having Jesus as an older brother.

But wait—I don't really have to imagine. Since I have been adopted into his family, he is my older brother. I had one other older brother, growing up, and we didn't always get along, but so far, Jesus has been perfect. I have disappointed him regularly, I'm afraid, but he always sticks up for me and is on my side. A real advocate. Who could ask for more?

I also got to thinking about my biological brother and when we were kids. He had a lot of different nicknames for me—some were his own; others were given by the family or neighbors. Colonel, Tornado Tom, Red, Carrot Top, the Menace—now that I give it a think, some of the names he called me were not suitable for printing. That, or I just don't want them to be known.

I wonder if Jesus has any nicknames for me, his little brother. I'm reminded again … "O ye of little faith."

I need to do something about that.

73

Escaping to the Right Place

I maneuvered my chair so that I could see only what I wanted to see—the flowers from a flower bed right in front of me. To my left was the grill, blocking most of the view of the house and neighbors' houses. To my right was our utility shed that blocked my view of the houses behind us. In front of me was a portion of our backyard and then, unfortunately, a fence and more yards and trees. I've positioned myself to block out as much as I can of a view that reminds me I live in a metropolitan area.

The problem is that even though I can't see it, I know it's there.

I have this problem in many areas. I try to block things out, but they're still there. The events of the past week —locally, nationally, and internationally—have left me wanting to bury my head in my arms and sing some nonsensible words so loud that I can't hear the news; can't hear the terrors around me.

Then, in a fit of responsibility, I feel I need to be informed, but every person has a different opinion and his or her own source of information. Who can be trusted? Then, every report has a differing view. Sites conflict, people fight, voices raise, criticism increases, anger rages ... I'm back to lowering my head and wanting to just escape.

Escape where? Wise words from the prophet Isaiah says to go to the teaching and the testimony (Isaiah 8:20). The answers as well as the truth are to be found in God's message. It's there that sense can be made, answers are given, and insights are revealed.

When I study, I find my responsibility is to love—that's it: love.

74

Daily Transformation

I learned something interesting this week. It has to do with actions and reactions—my own.

I am a Christian, and so when I act or react to something, I tend to think my reaction is Christian. I never realized how foolish this is. Just writing the first sentence in this paragraph is upsetting and unsettling.

The years-old practice of wearing "WWJD" bracelets always has bothered me. Too often, when someone does something great and honorable, the bracelet isn't even noticed. People should always do good, as Jesus always did good. But when a person who wears that bracelet does something irresponsible, it bothers me greatly. How could a person claim to be thinking, *What would Jesus do?*, and then act in a contrary way?

I came up with an idea. What about a "HCYDWJWDIYDKWHD" bracelet. The letters ask, "How can you do what Jesus would do if you don't know what he did." The challenge of the bracelet is to study the life of Christ to be able to understand him and know him, so you can discern, in any situation, what he would do.

But I find I do not have the inability to think fast enough to do what Jesus would do all the time. My thinking is too much like I

Craig Wagganer

mentioned before—I am a Christian, so however I react must be Christian as well. I am a follower of Christ, so when I do something, it must be what Jesus would have done.

I often act and react out of my humanity, rather than my Christianity. Worse, without thinking, I would assume they are congruent.

The instructions to the Old Testament kings of Israel were to make a copy of the Law and read from it daily (Deuteronomy 17:18–19). Concerning the life of Christ, what a transforming idea. And that's what I need—transformation.

75

Victorious Secret

Victoria's Secret sells intimate apparel. I want to get intimate but not about what you're wearing; rather, about what's inside.

If God were going to hide something, where would he hide it? If God had a mystery he wanted us to solve, how would he reveal it? Sometimes I feel like the Christian life is a divine game of hide-and-seek.

Colossians 1:27 gives us a glimpse. The mystery revealed is Christ in you, the hope of glory.

I think Christianity has tried to put the mystery in other places. Every denomination thinks the mystery, the secret, is locked up within its headquarters under the disguise of its particular doctrine or theology. Each sees itself as the keeper of the truth; in reality, aren't they all just franchises?

The mystery being revealed is Christ in the individual—discovering him there, cultivating his character, nurturing his spirit, and living the responsibility.

I see myself differently. I see others differently—each better, for Christ is there, the hope of glory.

76

My Own Little Sign

Dr. Martin Luther King Jr. wrote, "Without justice there can be no peace. He who passively accepts evil is as much involved in it as he who helps to perpetuate it." These are very wise and wonderfully challenging words that should call us all to action. Sir Edmund Burke is cited as having said, "All that is necessary for the triumph of evil is that good men do nothing." History should not be written out of silence. It is blasphemous to look back at history and see times when what is recorded is the result of good people doing nothing; a people passively accepting evil. Now cannot be one of those times.

But I think about myself and justice. I look back, thinking I never want justice. First, as a child, I didn't want justice; I wanted mercy. As I grew, as a teenager, I didn't want justice; I wanted mercy. As a husband, then father, and now grandfather, I don't want justice; I want mercy. As a brother, neighbor, friend, coworker, and even as a stranger, I don't want justice; I want mercy. I not only want mercy, but, from the depths my heart, I need mercy.

God by his nature demands justice. I beg for mercy. It is a terrifying situation ... until one stands in front of me, to protect me, and says he'll take the justice I deserve so that I can receive mercy.

So I come to the foot of the cross and lay down my own little sign: "Know Mercy, Know Peace."

77

The Dr. Seuss Conviction

I tend to be deliberate in decision making. When faced with important choices, I slow down and try to weigh everything. Sometimes I'm accused of being afraid, too cautious, or overly concerned with tangent considerations, but I am actually anxious about doing the right thing. And I wonder if God sometimes thinks that's comical.

One of the funniest verses in the Bible happens among the tragic events of Israel's exodus from Egypt. It plays out like a Dr. Seuss story. The second plague is upon Egypt, and frogs are absolutely everywhere. Pharaoh can't take it any longer and says to Moses, "Look over here and over there. The frogs—the frogs are everywhere. I open my eyes and look to see, and there are a million frogs in front of me. Frogs in the yard, and frogs in the street; squishy frogs beneath my feet. They're in my bed and all over the house, so much so I can't find my spouse. Help me, Moses. I can't take any more. These frogs have shaken me down to my core. The pain, the grief, and the tremendous sorrow! Get rid of these frogs ... but you can wait 'til tomorrow" (Exodus 8:8–10 MOV [My Own Version]).

Really? The plague has settled in, and frogs are everywhere. Pharaoh can't take it and pleads with Moses to call off the curse. Moses asks what I think is a silly question: "When do you want the plague to end?" And Pharaoh's response is, "Tomorrow." Really, Pharaoh? Tomorrow? Why not right now?

I read the story and wonder: if my conversations with God were recorded, might God add a laugh track to help convict me? Thinking back, sometimes I hear it.

78

Longing for the Day

There's a scene in the movie *Evan Almighty* where the lead character is shown a panorama of the subdivision where he lives, but the time was just after it was created. Beautiful hills and valleys were displayed in their original form, with a scenic beauty far beyond the present crowded landscape of houses, streets, and concrete.

I visited the gravesite where my brother, mother, and father are all buried. Rolling hills, plenty of trees, green grass disturbed only by rows of varying types of granite markers. I tried to picture it without the markers, as it was before it had been designated as a burial site.

Then I realized that one day it won't be a cemetery. Trying to visualize the scene before the markers were added made me think. Imagining it without the markers was looking into the future. Someday, the graves will be empty, and the old will be replaced with new. Second Peter says all this will melt away, and God will replace it with something new.

I wonder if in that kingdom, I will walk among this place with some who are currently buried there, and we'll discuss the victory achieved. The granite obelisks with names and dates will be replaced with smiling faces and songs of praise.

I can't wait.

79

Seed Power

We stopped by to see the grandchildren last night—almost ten years old, just turned seven years old, and two and a half years old. Amazing to see the differences, but also amazing to see the growth in each one—each starting as a little baby and the changes each time interval makes. Whether it's a few days, a month, or a year, change happens readily, quickly, and without permission. I recognized or realized that the changes are the product of potential and power.

Several times in the New Testament, Jesus refers to faith like a mustard seed. I had always interpreted that to mean faith as small as a mustard seed, but I see it differently now. When Jesus refers to faith like a mustard seed, he isn't referring to size but to power. Although the mustard seed is small, it will move soil and rocks and whatever is in its way to grow into a large seed-bearing plant. The bush, being much like a tree, is able to provide shade for people and nesting for birds.

It is a wonderful thing to observe the growth of children. It is inspiring and brings joy and happiness. From such a tiny beginning comes great things, and so much potential and opportunity awaits them. I think of my own children—they started as infants and now are wonderful examples of growth, potential, productivity, and social contributors and Christ followers. Something so small, but it wasn't their size; it was their power to become, to make a difference.

Simple Lessons Learned Along The Way

It makes a lot more sense that to move mountains, your faith needs to be as powerful as a mustard seed, not the size of one. When we look at a mustard seed, we shouldn't be amazed by its size but in awe of its power. My prayer is that when people look at me, they don't see the size of my faith, but are encouraged—even challenged—by the power.

80

A Sunny Destination

I was returning from an event in eastern Illinois. It was late evening when I came up a hill on Interstate 70. At the crest of the overpass, I saw an amazing sight. There was quite a crowd going west with me, and quite a few cars going east. The road we were crossing was also busy with cars going north and south. From this vantage point, I could see intersecting roads, and it seemed like there were people going in every direction.

As I looked up, I noticed all the vapor trails left by jets crisscrossing the sky. I wanted to count them, but keeping my eyes on the road while trying to count proved too difficult. Suffice it to say there were many.

I began to think of all the lives the cars and planes represented. I mused that this was an insignificantly small number compared to the rest of the world. All the people and all going somewhere. Planes, trains, automobiles …

I was lost in thought, considering all the destinations, the size of the world, and the people. All lives dwarfed by the size of the world but significant in the measure of their lives, families, and influence. But my thoughts drifted back to where everybody was going. I looked at cars and trucks and wondered what each story was. Then I began to wonder about my own story.

About that, I came around a slow curve, and as the road straightened, the sun was on the horizon immediately in front of me. It looked as if the road ran straight into the sun. I had my answer. My story is heading for the kingdom of God. There may be a lot to my story, just like each vehicle I encountered, but the final analysis—the final destination—is brighter than the sun. Full speed ahead.

81

Check with the Author First

Things have been happening that I'm not quite sure about. And some things don't happen, and I question that as well. Seems like life is just a series of steps from one situation or circumstance to the next. We make our plans, have our dreams, set our goals—and then life happens.

I meet a lot of people who have more questions than answers. Of course there are the whys and the what-nexts. But there are a whole lot more questions. Has it always been this way? It seems life used to be simpler, and maybe with all the technology and immediacy of things, life may be more complicated—or at least we're more aware.

A few years ago there was a V8 juice commercial that I loved. Decisions, decisions, and then a smack on the head—"I could have had a V8!"

I try to reason out my circumstances. I try to figure out why I'm in these situations. I try to understand what's going on and why. I search, I wonder, I ponder, I ask—and then it hits me: I could have had a V8!

The psalmist says it this way: "Let my cry come before you, O Lord; give me understanding according to your word" (Psalm 119:169).

Simple Lessons Learned Along The Way

For answers to life, I need go to the author. His Word is the original thinking, not outside the box but way beyond it, with creative and real solutions to all the illusions that would otherwise distract me or bury me in my own foolish thinking or wisdom of this world.

May the author of my life come to be always the first source and destination of my search.

82

Seeking Mission Wisdom

I had a few minutes to kill, so I grabbed a book off the shelf and went outside to sit for a while and read. The book was a little devotional-type that I hadn't looked at for a few years. I opened it, randomly found a chapter, and began to read. It was the third time in recent weeks that I was confronted about having personal mission and vision statements.

I came back inside and found the notebook where I'd begun this endeavor—several times—over the past many years. I never get it quite done. Nothing ever sounds noble, wise, or sincere enough. I want to do it, but it just doesn't happen. There are formulas to help, but that seems so artificial. Maybe it is a mental block, maybe mental problems ... I don't know. I just can't seem to get it down.

What would be interesting would be to interview some of the people who know me best, who observe my life, and who are active participants in my living and ask them to write the mission and vision statements that I portray. Maybe what I consider my mission to be isn't as important as what others would observe it to be.

In Acts 13:36, Paul observes about King David that he served the purposes of God in his generation. Peter says, concerning Paul, that although his writings may be difficult, and he said it in many ways, the message of Paul was to count the patience of our Lord as salvation (2 Peter 3:15–16).

Maybe a good time of devotion would be to spend time with God, not asking him what my mission is but asking if what he observes—and what others observe—is pleasing.

83

Mowing Spirituality

My neighbor is out of town for a few days. Just before he and his wife left, they got word that their air conditioner was almost dead. Right after that, they found a leak in a water pipe in their basement. The leak has been going on for a while and has caused some damage, not to mention a very expensive repair. All this news kept them busy up until the time they left, and so he lamented not getting his grass cut.

Today, I went out to cut my grass. I looked at my neighbor's and thought I'd be a good neighbor and cut his grass too. The yards aren't big, and I can cut mine in an hour, so his would double that—no worries, right? I had some time, and he'd really be glad not to have that job when he got back.

His yard is nicer than mine, or at least the grass is thicker. It was heavy to cut, and since I use a bagger, I had to empty it about every two passes in his yard. The cutting was easy, but emptying the bag and restarting my old mower was a little laborious. In my yard, I have to empty the bag once in the front and three times in the back. The neighbor's was about twelve to fifteen times in the back.

Now, I don't begrudge him what I did, but maybe you have found this to be true—you start out to do a good deed, and it quickly becomes more than you thought. But your desire was sincere, and so you do the favor, and it all turns out well. The neighbors' yard looks nice, and I am sure they will appreciate the effort.

Now I get to lie. I don't want him to know I did it, or he will wind up doing mine sometime, thinking he has to return the favor. I didn't do it as an investment. I did it to be nice. I didn't do because I had to or felt indebted. I did it because I wanted to. I do not want any obligatory response. I know how it can feel to return from time away and find work that has piled up. I wanted to take one thing off their plate, and I was in the position to help.

Proverbs 3:27 is good advice: "Do not withhold good from those to whom it is due, when it is in your power to do it."

84

My Septic Perspective

I read a story this week that reminded me of an incident concerning a friend several years ago.

He was pastoring a church in Ohio that was undergoing major renovations. These updates included adding much-needed bathroom space and new sidewalks. There was quite a discussion with local authorities on the additional septic system, how it was to be constructed, and all the regulations and permits that would be necessary. Also, various soil samples would have to be submitted, with additional studies on drainage and ground quality surrounding the area.

It was a very lengthy process in which plans were submitted, not accepted, resubmitted and not accepted again, redesigned and not approved, and then completely revamped. Finally, approval was given so the site could be developed. Stern warning was given that once the site was prepared, it would have to be approved, and at that point further revisions would probably be necessary.

The site was prepared, and all the necessary studies and reports were filed. The proper permits were displayed, and time came for an inspector to come out and approve the site. It had been such a lengthy, drawn-out, detailed process that the church people were very concerned about what the on-site visual inspection might reveal and what additional changes would be needed.

On the day of the inspection, several people waited nervously for the inspector. There were still various projects going on with the addition, but this was crucial to be able to proceed. Tensions were high, and tempers were on edge when the inspector finally arrived and exited his vehicle.

He walked toward the gathered men. He looked over the site and bent down to look at the elevation from several angles. He said very little besides introducing himself and stating he was in a hurry. He took some notes, signed a paper, and told them they had done a great job and could continue to finish the system; they had their approval.

He returned to his vehicle and was off quickly, presumably to his next inspection.

The group of church members now had another dilemma: the site for which the inspector gave final approval for a new septic system was actually the forms for a new sidewalk, about a hundred yards from the septic system.

Too often I am not sure how God is working, and I question things from my own limited perspective. I need to remember Isaiah 55:8-9. God sees from the fully informed perspective. Even when I cannot see the hand of God, I can trust his heart. I'm praying for a heart of wisdom.

85

No More Lost Days

It has been almost two weeks since I had surgery—eleven days, actually.

I don't know what happened to or during that time. The days are gone, and although I have vague memories of the pain and recovery that I am still enduring, I find myself at a loss to actually recount the days.

As I have felt better, I have started going back into my office to work on projects that I had begun before going under the knife. I find I can't make sense of my notes, and many of the projects seem like a jigsaw puzzle I can't piece together. My organized pile of notes and open books seem a strange mess left by someone else. I try to think back, reassemble, and reconstruct, but it just doesn't seem to work.

I've never had surgery before, and I don't like it. It has truly messed up my life. I am still weak and get tired much too easily—which also means I get frustrated easily when I try to start putting things back together. My wonderful wife assures me I am getting better every day, in which case I am looking forward to several years from now, but for now, it is all very debilitating.

The psalmist asked the Lord to help us number our days that we may attain a heart of wisdom. Maybe the wisdom is that as we count our days, we learn to make each day count.

86

Reflected Image

Whenever we're together with the grandkids, it seems it always comes up—who do they look like? Usually, the conversation has each one looking like somebody when he or she makes a certain expression and another somebody when a different expression is made. Then we'll get on to their actions—who do they act like?

So in appearance it may depend on the expression, but with activities, it may depend on good or bad. Usually it starts as a reflection on the parents and then grandparents. There are some definite genealogical traits. We can trace them back on each side of the families.

Sometimes when we go through pictures, we see dominant traits that seem to show up every generation. Other times, we see generations-old pictures and notice something in the grandkids that we didn't see before. Oftentimes we'll hear and tell stories about ancestors and then realize the same attitudes or expressions are still being carried on. Even very small, unconscious activities can remind us of generations past.

When all the talk is over, the comparisons made, and the similarities discussed, the point is finally made—each one is a unique individual, even though there may be connections in image and attitude.

Craig Wagganer

Jesus once said to render to Caesar that which has Caesar's image and to God that which has God's image. In the beginning, God made man in his image. My traits, physical and otherwise, may reveal part of my heritage. But I pray that my real image will reflect the one in whose image I was created and that people will readily recognize him in my genealogy.

87

Unseen Influence

I saw an interesting science trick. You take a few small candles, place them in a row, and then light them. You then take a small glass and put in a little baking soda and vinegar—not enough to produce a volcano but just so it bubbles; I don't know the exact amounts.

Being careful not to tip the glass too far and pour out the liquid, you slightly tip the glass over the candles, and the flames will be extinguished. The vinegar and the baking soda produce carbon dioxide, which is heavier than air and remains in the glass just above the liquid. When you tip the glass over, you pour the carbon dioxide out and invisibly extinguish the flames.

The flames are extinguished, but the source that puts the flames out isn't discernible.

Paul states in 1 Corinthians 15:33 that we should not be confused; bad company corrupts good morals. Our flame can be put out by unseen forces if we are not aware of the influences around us.

88

Childish Learning

A few months ago our neighbors across the street suffered a house fire. It was an alarming and scary time. Since then, there's been a succession of people working on the house to get it back to a livable condition. It's been almost totally rebuilt.

It has been interesting to see the different people involved in working on the house. Many different trucks, different types of trucks, and a lot of different people, all with different skills and abilities, coming to work to make the house ready for the family to move back in. The house appears to be approaching completion.

When I think about my life, I see that there have been so many influences that have contributed to who I am. So many people come and make contributions to who I am and who I am becoming; they are involved in building or rebuilding me. The interesting thing is that some are invited and some aren't, but the influence is still there.

This past week I was thinking about the influences that have been strong in the past couple of years. There is one who has challenged me, worried me, and contributed more than any other to my growth and development. My wonderful and beautiful daughter, Annie, is one of the most influential people in my life. She is a professor of sociology at a local college and always brings a fresh perspective, a creative challenge, and humorous insight. She amazes me.

Isaiah 59:21 says that our offspring shall have the Spirit and words of the Lord. Most assuredly, my children are my teachers.

Seems like I am always evaluating my life, and I don't always get good grades. But I am getting better, I know, because Annie is in my life.

89

Planted Fruit

I learned a long time ago about sowing and reaping. Three truths: (1) what you sow is what you reap; (2) you reap after you sow; and (3) you reap more than you sow. These three truths have been in my heart as I'm constantly reminded—and need to be reminded—to be careful what I sow. I usually think of this in the context of my activity; that is, my sowing and subsequent reaping.

But today I had a different—perhaps paradoxical—thought. God has sown things in me, and he expects to reap. Second Corinthians 5 says that we have been reconciled and so given the ministry of reconciliation. He sowed our new relationship with him through Jesus and expects us to share with others that opportunity. So what else has been sown in me that needs to produce a harvest?

He has given me love that I didn't deserve, joy I can't understand, peace that satisfies, patience beyond my own ability, kindness when I deserved judgment, goodness when I haven't been, faithfulness that is like a mighty tree, gentleness that holds me, and self-control to abide in me. He has sown these in me. What will he reap?

Everything I learn about God, about what he's done and his desires for me, is the planting of those virtues into my soul. If I take them to heart and nurture them within the fertile ground of my being, they will produce a harvest in my character and activities.

Maybe that's why they're called fruit (Galatians 5:23).

90

An Awkward Situation

I was selected to go through the TSA security as "pre-checked" as I left St. Louis for San Francisco. That meant I could leave my belt, shoes, and glasses on. I placed my backpack on the conveyor and proceeded through the metal detector.

My first time through the alarm sounded, and I was instructed to take off my belt and try again. I placed my belt in a little bowl and walked through the detector again. Beeps went off, and I was instructed to take off my glasses and try again. This time, I was cleared. By this time the conveyor coming out of the x-ray machine was backed up from the people waiting behind me.

I found my glasses and belt among the personal items of others along the conveyor. At the very end was my backpack, with a suitcase that looked just like mine, except mine is brown, and this one was black. I did a quick scan to see if I could find the person who had taken my bag and left his. No one in sight.

I called attention to a TSA agent, who brought an assistant over the help. They inspected the suitcase and checked it thoroughly. There was quite a discussion of someone taking my bag by mistake and leaving his own on the conveyor. They announced over the terminal public address system that the person who had left his bag at security should return to claim it.

Simple Lessons Learned Along The Way

A few moments later, a young woman approached to claim her bag. She identified the bag, and the security agents identified her as the owner. She was asked about taking the wrong bag, but she hadn't; she had just forgotten to take her bag off the conveyor. She was questioned but obviously had no idea about my suitcase.

TSA began to question me, making sure I had gone through that particular line. What to do next? You may have already figured out the problem after reading what I placed on the conveyor, before the scanner fiasco.

I had a moment of realization. I put one hand on the shoulder of one agent and the other hand on the other agent's shoulder. I asked if I could buy them a cup of coffee or any drink they preferred or perhaps a snack of some type. They both responded negatively with a questioning look in their eyes. I offered again, saying I would really, really like to do something special for them. They continued to decline, and then I thanked them for their attention to my problem and asked for forgiveness as I confessed what I had just remembered—I had checked my bag.

We laughed—or they laughed—and said they were just glad to have it settled. I again made my offer and again asked for forgiveness. The offer was declined but forgiveness granted. We talked about the coincidence of someone's leaving a bag that looked like mine and that if the poor woman had not left her bag, I would not have thought about mine.

I am grateful that God promises to forgive my sins upon my confession (1 John 1:9), whether they are intentional or not, whether they involve others or not. But upon any realization, I need to confess. Sometimes, certainly not always, I even get a laugh out of it. I imagine God does too.

91

The Hills Are Alive

Last week's travel to San Francisco brought an enlightening reminder.

The day I arrived was cloudy. During the night, it began to rain, which continued through most of the next day. The day I left for the airport was cloudy. The atmospheric conditions left me unable to see sun, moon, or stars during my entire stay.

As I was returning to the airport, I was thinking about the clouds. At first I was dismayed that the clouds had blocked the sun the whole trip. The scenery was beautiful, and how much more so it would have been if the sun had been shining. Then I thought, *It was only because of the brightness of the sun that I was able to see the clouds.*

In 2 Kings 6, the Syrian army surrounds the man of God. His faithful aide is very much afraid, while the prophet remains calm. With fear mounting, the prophet eases the aide's anxiousness by stating that those who are with them greatly outnumber those who are against them. Eyes are opened revealing the army of the Lord encompassing and protecting the man of God and his helper.

I don't think that when the army of the Lord arrived that it was seen by one and not the other; rather, the prophet knew they were there without seeing them. The vision revealed to the aide confirmed what the prophet already knew.

Thanksgiving? I'm thankful for the presence of God even when—especially when—he may seem hidden. For it is the very presence of God that illuminates circumstances that may otherwise seem he has disappeared.

92

Blazing a Trail

I was looking up at the sky on a sunny day and noticed the vapor trails of jets that had crossed the sky. They went in every direction. The planes were long gone, traveling at their exceptional rates of speed, but the vapor trails remained.

The jets fly across the sky, and the trail begins as a small stream coming from the engines, but then that vapor begins to enlarge and grow into what might even appear as a stretched-out cloud. By then, the jet is out of sight; only a vapor remains.

It causes a simple prayer: "Lord, may my presence bring love and encouragement. And when others have left my presence may a vapor of influence remain to brighten their days. If any good comes, may it be to your glory and your praise, for it is your presence and your love that began the good work" (Philippians 1:6; 2:13).

93

Seeking a Glimpse

Sitting in the window seat on a recent trip, I found myself staring out the window. I had read, my eyes were tired, and I couldn't concentrate. I took out a magazine and thumbed through the articles. I pulled out my MP3 player and listened to some songs of my brother's, recorded a year or two before he passed away. I found myself thinking about him and listening to his music.

As we jetted along, it was a kind of cloudy day, but once in a while there would be a break in the clouds, and I would get a glimpse of a city some thirty thousand feet below. I began looking for and anticipating the breaks in the clouds so I could see what we were flying over. Sometimes I could see a city, other times little towns. We passed over the Rocky Mountains. We passed over areas where I couldn't even find a road. We had long periods of just clouds.

Life is shrouded in sin. The contamination has come upon the world, and the reaping of what has been sown is devastating. We see it all around us, and it clouds our vision. Somehow it hides the promise of God's kingdom.

But once in a while, we see a vision of the coming kingdom. The clouds are rolled back and separated. We see glimpses of the love of God vividly displayed, and our hope is renewed. We experience the Spirit that was given as a down payment toward our coming inheritance. Hope is alive, and faith is renewed; love prevails.

I hear people quote the little verse from 1 Corinthians 2. "What no eye has seen, nor ear heard, nor the heart of man imagined, what God has prepared for those who love Him" I call it a little verse because the verse the follows is the big one: "These things God has revealed to us through His spirit." I find myself praying for these revelations. I pray for the clouds to be cleared. Maybe that's what seeking the kingdom first is all about (Matthew 6:33).

94

Easier with My Father

It was a pretty easy assignment: build a screech-owl nesting box. It was a project at my grandson's Cub Scout meeting. The six pieces of wood and the screws for construction were provided; all we needed to bring was a power screwdriver.

Ben and I gathered the pieces and began construction. It was pretty simple: lay the pieces together and begin screwing the boards together. The problem was that the power drill was a little heavy for Ben to control by himself. The basic lesson was to make sure the boards were aligned, put the screw in the pilot hole, hold the drill straight with the screw, pull the trigger, and apply pressure. This is easier for a grandpa to explain than for a grandson to manage.

So we would set up the pieces, getting everything ready. I would support the drill in the right position, and he would grab the handle and pull the trigger. After the first couple of tries, he caught on quickly, and we completed the house with ease.

It was an amazing adventure. He did a little work, but he thought he was contributing much more than he did in reality. It was my alignment, supporting the drill's weight, helping with the pressure, and knowing when to signal him to pull and let off the trigger. But Ben helped and was so very proud. Once it was completed, we

Craig Wagganer

hugged, and he thanked me generously and started talking about other projects we could do together.

How unseen and how overwhelming is the help of my Father's hand every day. He aligns me, supporting the weight I cannot, He knows how much pressure to apply, and he motivates me. More than that, he holds me and receives my thanks when I remember to give it.

So glad to be in the Father's hands (Isaiah 49:15–16).

95

A Watery Lesson

I was out of coffee filters, so I got out the Keurig. I readied the water and the coffee and was waiting for the water to pass through the K-Cup. For that short moment of waiting, I wondered how the water felt about the situation. The water, which is fine all by itself, is heated, put under pressure, and passed through another substance that transforms it into something completely different. Is the water okay with this process, or is it offended?

I have gone through—am going through, and will continue to go through in the future—situations that change me. Each situation is ordained by God to test me and change me for his purpose and for use as an instrument for his kingdom. Oftentimes I see with limited perspective and hate the situation, seeing it as an incident rather than his formula.

I enjoy coffee. Hot water? Not so much. For me, the process of using hot water to make coffee is worth the effort and sacrificing the natural state of the water.

I pray that when I pass through situations that the filter brings me out pleasing to God.

May I understand that he is trying to finish my brewing (Psalm 119:71; 1 Peter 1:6–7).

96

A Daily Gift

I sat at my desk, brought the computer back from sleeping, and waited for a program to load. While sitting there, I noticed some wrapping paper on the edge of my desk. It's been resting there since Christmas.

My mind wandered, and I clicked on the "pictures" tab on my computer and began looking at photos I had taken when the family was together for our Christmas celebration at the cabin.

One of the pictures caught my attention and imagination. On the morning when we open gifts, we set them all out and arrange them according to for whom they are intended; each person has his or her own pile of gifts. After they're arranged, before they are assaulted, I take a picture of the gifts waiting to meet their new owners.

In that picture, everything was neatly arranged, stacked in an almost artistic display. The scene is quiet, except for the anticipation of the grand unveiling. All is ready, just waiting, waiting, waiting ...

Every day God begins by setting an unlimited number of wrapped presents before us—opportunities, experiences, relationships, feelings. The day is wrapped, new and fresh, bringing our anticipation of what will happen.

Another series of pictures showed each person unwrapping the gifts prepared for him or her. It's fun looking back, but you know, not all the presents were winners. Some were just so-so, and others brought a hidden response of *What?*

But each gift received is gratefully acknowledged and everyone feels good about what was given and received. Hidden wonders remain hidden, love is experienced, and even some tears of joy are shed.

I often move through my days mundanely. It's just another day. I keep moving, going through the motions, with little expectation—too little joy and too busy to notice.

"God, please help me to realize each new day as a neatly wrapped gift from you. May I enter with joyful anticipation and faithful expectations of your presence and each opportunity and experience as your present to me. And at the close of the day, regardless of how well I have taken advantage of or even noticed all the gifts you have given, let my heart recount the day with praise and adoration for letting me unwrap the gifts I found, and let me be forgiven for what I overlooked. Please give me another chance and help me to do better."

97

In the "Q"

I had a query. I read the word "quark" and wasn't sure what it meant. I looked it up and found it is a scientific term for the smallest form of matter. It's what atoms are made of. One definition said that quarks are the building blocks of life.

I began to think about the building blocks of life. We see life from our own perspectives. We have no choice. We can work to change our perspectives, and we all have enlightening moments when our paradigms change. But even when we change, even when we have new perspectives, they are our perspectives.

We see things according to the sum of our experiences and personalities and other ingredients in our lives. The sum total of my foibles, failures, talents, gifts, circumstances, successes, my very best, my very worst—all the quirks that make me *me*. These are the ingredients that God uses to help me understand who I am and what I am to be.

So the question I am facing is this; are the things that distinctly make me and the pressures and problems I am currently facing the building blocks that God is using to help me determine the reason for my existence?

So my query is this: are my quirks the quarks that will define my quest? I think yes. So I must ruminate on the quirks, for they are the quarks God is using to deliver me into his kingdom.

98

Amram's Legacy

Oftentimes the most little-noted person is one who has a major influence. A person's influence is in no way related to the accolades or recognition he or she may get. And the most influential people—the ones who are making a constant difference in people's lives and in the world—don't do it for recognition. Their contributions are a matter of their hearts, their characters, and their values.

Most of us are familiar with the story of Moses. As a child, he was hidden in the river until the daughter of Pharaoh, Bithia, came upon him. Moses's older sister watched and then told Bithia she knew of a Hebrew nurse for the child, and Jochebed, Moses's mother, was called to be a nurse and help raise the child.

We often speculate as to Jochebed's influence, and it is undeniable. But after Moses reached his fame and led the Hebrews out of slavery across the Red Sea, and Pharaoh's armies were destroyed, Moses briefly recognized another major influence.

In Exodus 15, Moses became the first recorded songwriter and recognized the Lord's triumph. But in the fourth line of the song, he made quite a statement: "This is my God, and I will praise him, my father's God, and I will exalt him."

Craig Wagganer

Little is known of Amram, but Moses recognized his father's faith in this little line of song, written of God's triumph over the cruelty of the Egyptians. Jochebed, we know, was directly involved in Moses's childhood, but apparently, so was his father, and his father's faith was an ingredient in Moses's faith.

Looking back, I clearly recognize the role of my father's faith in my life. I can only pray that by the grace of God, my faith has a positive impact for my children.

99

Credit to the Source

I gave a gift to a friend. I knew it was something he wanted but couldn't afford. It wasn't big or very expensive, and I was glad to be able to make the contribution. I did it anonymously, so there wouldn't be any refusing or need for payback. It made me feel good.

A short time after the gift was given, the person approached me and said how thrilled he was with what he had received. He then said he knew who had been so gracious to him. He described all the clues and his understanding of the situation, and he came to the conclusion of who had given him the gift. His conclusion was wrong; he gave someone else the credit for what I had done.

There have been times when I have looked at someone who is extremely gifted with a tremendous amount of ability and talent, but he or she gave no glory or credit to God. In fact, at times the person even denies the existence of the One who made him or her with such extreme abilities. It causes me to have questions.

My friend, to whom I gave a gift, didn't recognize me as the giver of the gift. But that didn't change the fact that I was the one. Even though another may have received credit, I was still the giver of the gift.

The fact that someone might deny that his or her talent and abilities come from God or even just ignore the fact does not change that it was God who gave generously. Although a great musician, a gifted mechanic, a wonderful organizer, a beautiful dancer, or a supreme entertainer may not give glory to God for his or her talent, it in no way makes God less responsible.

When Bezalel and Oholiab were chosen as master craftsmen for the building of the tabernacle in Exodus 35, I wonder how many other talented people might have been available for the job. But there must have been a reason these two were filled with the Holy Spirit. Maybe they recognized the source of their abilities.

100

One More Thing

Second Corinthians 8 tells the story of people who were extremely generous. Paul, who relates the story, tells how they went beyond what was expected of them. A couple of words struck my curiosity: "expected but ..." In this case, the reference is to people who did what was expected but also went beyond that and did more; they exceeded expectations.

I suppose the words could be used negatively. "They did what was expected but grudgingly"—or some other rendering of people who do what is expected but that's all, or perhaps with attitude or behavior that detracts from the expectation.

Jesus died, was buried, and was resurrected for us. If no other thing was done, that alone should exceed our expectations. But he gave us blessing upon blessing after that; to enumerate would be impossible. I can't even give examples—words fail to explain the wonder I feel.

Exceeding expectations, going the extra mile, giving above and beyond—that's the example to live by.

About the Author

Craig Wagganer is a disciple of Jesus Christ who masquerades as an entrepreneur, business owner, and author. He lives in St. Louis with his wife, Shirley. They have a wonderful son, Zachary, who is married to his charming wife, Annie Michelle. They also have a fantastic daughter, Annie Marie. Craig and Shirley have three grandchildren: Hannah, Benjamin, and Sarah. All of the family lives in St. Louis, providing inspiration for Craig's work.

Craig is available for seminars, workshops, and as a keynote or guest speaker. You can contact him through his website, LeadersBridge.com.